# Unlock Your True Potential

*Believe and Achieve the Impossible!*

by

Salvatore Bruno

Grosvenor House
Publishing Limited

This book is published by
Grosvenor House Publishing Ltd
Link House
140 The Broadway, Tolworth, Surrey, KT6 7HT.
www.grosvenorhousepublishing.co.uk

A CIP record for this book
is available from the British Library

ISBN 978-1-83975-278-0

# CONTENTS

# CONTENTS

# CONTENTS

# INTRODUCTION

My name is Salvatore Bruno, and I welcome you to my book.

I invite you to join me as we take this journey on how to prepare for a better and brighter future.

We will look at how we use the negatives and positives from the past to fuel us in the present, allowing us to push forward into the future.

I will share my tips, my views on how I see life, overcoming life's hurdles, and how to choose the right paths for you. But most of all, how to believe in yourself and to overcome the impossible while becoming the best version of yourself.

Come join me as I share my stories on how I look at life, how I became the man I am today, and how I overcame my impossible challenges.

We all have a gift in being able to make our own choices; it's your choice if you want to see life through positive eyes and to live life your way... It's time to unlock your true potential.

It just comes down to one question: Are you ready?

# Chapter 1
# WHERE IT ALL BEGAN!

Where did it all start for me? Well, I was born in Slough in Berkshire in the United Kingdom, in September of 1976 – the year some people remember due to the summer being one of the hottest on record. Of course, that was before we destroyed the planet (that subject is for another book!); now we are breaking all sorts of weather records.

Are you old enough to remember those years? A time when the world was completely different: no social media; no WhatsApp; no Skype. In fact, we didn't have mobile phones back then. And the internet? What was that?

Life was simple. If you wanted to know where someone was, you got off your arse and looked for them. If you rang someone on the house phone and they weren't at home, you couldn't get hold of them until they got back. And I'm not talking about using flash cordless phones. Oh no, I am talking about the corded ones which meant you had to stand or sit in the same place while you were on a call.

Letters were a big thing back then, too. Remember them? If you don't, those are bits of paper which you wrote on and then stuck in an envelope and posted. That's right, you had to actually write on paper and then walk to a red box outside your house or at the post office, then the letter would arrive at the other end a few days later. Well, we hoped it did. Post: incredible, right?

Another thing back then was, if you wanted to know if someone was ok, you asked them to their face. Yes, their face! Not a message, or dm, or something written on the Facebook wall; you actually had to make conversation, because TV was not a great thing to watch. There was no Netflix or Amazon Prime. Imagine trying to get five people around a tiny black and white TV. Yip, you heard me, black and white.

The world we live in today feels millions of years different to the one back then, when life felt a lot simpler, but in a flick of a coin a very difficult one. Being brought up by two European parents had its ups and downs. Most of my family were living in Spain or Italy – even some in Canada – while most of my friends were British and all their family was around the corner. It meant we had to wait until our holidays to see our relatives.

Don't get me wrong. I was brought up by amazing parents and we had a great family bond.

My mum still lives in the same family home where my brother and sister and I all grew up.

But it was the little things that affected me: the way my name would stand out on the school register; and feeling like an outsider for most of my school life. To be honest, I didn't help myself by taking years to learn how to spell it, ha-ha! I even went down the route of being bullied for a while.

It was a hard time, and to be honest there are some real dark memories. Being bullied for no other reason apart from having a name that sounded different, seems wrong, doesn't it? But it happened. And once you start going down that path, it's a hard one to get out of. You will never understand that feeling of being bullied unless you have been there, and it starts so quickly and comes out of the blue.

It begins with just words or maybe a small punch, or it can start full-on. But either way, school life becomes difficult.

Also, back then, teachers had no idea about dyslexia, so the pupils who struggled just got moved to a table or classroom for what I would call the "stupid kids". Don't worry, I know what it was like. I was one of them.

But this is not a sad story; this is not about me naming the people that affected my life as a child in a negative way. I just want to explain that I am just a normal guy who learnt from life lessons and made use of them. This is me saying that some of you may have walked down the same path I did, or are currently going through it now.

I know so many people that went through a hard time at school but never talked about until later on in life. And I know so many people who became stronger and stronger the more times they were pushed into the corner. Some are still affected by how they lived back then, and it has affected them for years. But most of the people I know used that experience and decided to improve their life. They took a different path and are now heading in a direction that makes them smile and super happy.

In saying that, it's not the dark memories that I remember; it's the fun ones – the ones that impacted my life one way or another.

So, this is about saying that everyone's path starts somewhere. It doesn't matter if you wanted it to happen or not, but the moment you are born you are put on a path. Some children come into this world with amazing parents and a beautiful roof over their heads and others don't.

The choice of what country or area you grow up in is made for you, as is what school you go to, the religion you are born into, the colour of your skin, and even down to if you are born male or female. All of these are things you have no control over, which means you are born and put on a path of life. Is it a good path? Is it amazing? Or is it a bad path?

It's only later on in life, as we start to grow up, that we are taught to start making choices: who we hang out with; what subjects we want to learn; what sports to play; what clothes to wear. But we are still restricted in what we can and can't do.

Look at it this way: your parents are into football. Now, I am talking about real football nutters, you know the ones I mean – they truly love it, all they do is talk about it, football this, football that. And then you are born... what do you think your parents are going to try and teach you?

So you see, the path of life is very much a true thing, and as a child, you are just going along for the ride. It can take years to see it or even be able to change it; it can take years to realise what you want to do, that it's your choice, it's your path, your journey.

It has to be said, though, I know some people who still just go along for the ride. They have no real dreams, no plans to improve their life or themselves.

Have you ever thought to yourself that you were born into the wrong life, that the path chosen for you was wrong from the beginning? It's amazing the number of people walking this planet who will agree that they are one of those people. Millions, even billions, of people on the wrong path!

*'SOMETIMES LIFE WILL PUT YOU ON THE WRONG PATH, BUT THE GREAT THING ABOUT LIFE'S PATH IS THAT IT HAS MANY FORKS AND CROSSROADS ALONG THE WAY.'*

*Salvatore Bruno*

This is why I like to explain this to all parents I see. Sometimes they don't realise they are pushing their children down a path which may be causing the child issues, and forcing them down a road which could be a problem later on. Maybe after you have read this, and you are a parent, you can think about your children's path of life. Picture yourself going along it: how would you change it?

Think of the film *Billy Elliot*, which is set in North East England during the 1984-85 coal miners' strike. The film stars Jamie Bell as 11-year-old Billy, an aspiring dancer dealing with the negative stereotype of the male ballet dancer; Gary Lewis as his coal miner father; Jamie Draven as Billy's bullying older brother.

Imagine if we had a machine at birth that would allow us to choose who we were and what path we went down. Would you be where you are now? Would you be the person you are today?

*Question:*

*If you had a time machine and could go back to your childhood, what would you change? And what would you say would impact you the most by this change?*

# Chapter 2

# IS IT REAL OR FAKE?!

The world nowadays is a very different place, and sometimes it's hard to know what is real or fake. It is a fine line between what people see on social media and what is real life, because people lie, hide the truth, or just show people what they want people to see.

Some people take 10 selfies just to get that perfect picture – the ones where filters are used, the right lighting, even Photoshop. Is this bad? Is this wrong? I hope not, as I have done all of the above.

People who are not happy in themselves can now get joy by having someone liking their picture or status. You also get those people who post those updates about how bad their day is, how awful life is. We all have a friend who does that. It doesn't make them wrong, or does it?

Then on the other side of the coin, we get the others that will write about how amazing life is and how perfect their job is, but really their life sucks and their manager is a complete prat who gives them a hard time for no reason, but they haven't got it in them to leave and look for a new job. And yep, I also did and have been there as well.

Of course, there are some people who don't use social media at all, and there is nothing wrong with that. I guess it depends what you want out of life.

I have friends that live in a beautiful finca in the heart of the Andalucía hills. They wake up every morning to blue skies and are surrounded by breathtaking views... but they hate social media.

They are happy with the land around them and don't care what the rest of the world thinks or know about them.

Me? I have grown with the times, using the internet to improve my lifestyle and knowledge, plus using the great apps to keep in contact with friends and family around the world. When I was younger, my family didn't know what I was doing or how we were. I remember the days that my parents would stand in the hallway for hours talking on the telephone to my family in other countries, timing it so that all the relatives were at my uncle's or grandparents' house. Now the world is a small place, and communication can be kept up easily. No matter where they may be, my family can see my life and everything I care to share via different social media outlets.

Remember when you could make a video call for the first time? It blew my parents away. Suddenly, they could now have a conversation and see the person at the same time.

This has made our huge world into a small one, now that we can stay connected, But it has also allowed the world to separate and divide people. In my eyes, the world is a changed place now, and it's very hard to know if the 'John Smith' who just liked my picture or who sent me a Facebook request, is actually a John Smith.

I still find the best way to meet real people is by getting out there and talking. I am lucky enough to travel a lot which means I spend a fair time in airports, and that is one of the best places to meet people. There, you have something in common and people are a lot more open to talking. Why? Because most of them are going on holiday or a business trip, so normally the first question is: 'Where you heading?' or 'Where you off to?'

We don't know these people, but we're happy to tell them our life story, where we are going, and what our plans are. But if someone passing you on the street asked you where you were going on holiday, you wouldn't be so open to tell them.

So, I use face-to-face connection, but also still use the internet and social media to network with new people. Some of my good friends I have met by networking over social media. It's just a massive trust thing nowadays whether they are real or fake, and sometimes you have no way of knowing until it's too late.

### Question:

*If someone looked you up on your social media, would they see the real you or the fake you?*

# Chapter 3

# THE PATHS WITHIN
# THIS WORLD!

Once you have answered the last question honestly
to yourself, it takes us to the next step; it takes us
to the paths within this world. And this is super-
important to know: you will always need direction,
and you need to know where you want to be.

Don't get me wrong. I have had people in the
past turn around to me and say, 'I don't care where
I end up.'

And let's be honest, those people will never read
a book like this. I just want people to be open-
minded to the fact that they can take control and
choose the path they want, but to do this you will

need strength and determination to get what you want. It won't be easy, but it will be worth it.

Before we start on learning how to find the correct paths, you need to understand that you may make mistakes, and you may take the wrong paths before you find the right one. The reason I say that is because that is the way it goes.

Anyone who says they can find the perfect path for you is lying. You will have to find it, and before you even start to look, you need to have a direction, a target, so to speak. For some strange reason, I find a lot of people start to worry when I talk about targets, goals, dreams, etc. It's like the moment I say these words, they immediately put pressure on themselves. But that is the wrong thing to do. No pressure is needed if you do this right.

So, now I am going to put out some facts in front of you. Some of you will read them and say to yourself, 'I know this already.' Others may read them and understand the changes they need to make to their day-to-day life but don't know how.

Changing your mindset doesn't have to be difficult. It's about understanding the simple facts:

- Life can be improved.
- Money isn't everything.
- You can choose your path.
- You never stop learning.
- You can always improve yourself.
- It's never too late to learn from your mistakes.
- You can always make a positive from a negative.
- The impossible is possible.
- We are humans so we can adapt to new things.

Sound stupid?

You probably read that list and thought to yourself, *I know that!* Well, if you did, then it won't take a lot to improve your life... unless you are lying to yourself and you say you're doing it when you're only doing it 50% or less.

*'IF YOU WANT TO IMPROVE YOUR LIFE YOU MUST RESPECT ONE RULE, NEVER LIE TO YOURSELF.'*

*Paulo Coelho*

The biggest questions of all are: are you willing to improve your life for yourself? Are you willing to become the better version of yourself for you, your friends, and family? Because if you are willing, there is nothing stopping you from changing paths and improving your life.

I write that as if it's so easy to do, like crossing the road, but guess what? It is. It is as simple as flipping a coin.

The difference is your outlook on your future and how you see the paths of life. You see, life will knock you down, kick you to the kerb, and try to wash you into the gutter. And when this happens, you feel like it can't get any better, life is over, or you just say to yourself that this is how life is meant to be.

I do understand these feelings. I have been there a few times for all different reasons, and there is nothing nice about being in that dark place. It's crap, you feel like the world is against you, you can't see any light at the end of the tunnel, you feel that you are the only person in the world this is happening to, and you truly believe there is no way back.

I have seen it affect people in different ways. Some do silly things, reacting in ways we wouldn't normally do and saying things that we wouldn't normally say. That's because when you are in that dark place, you can't see how you are and how you are reacting. Others tell you, but you can't hear them.

This is why sometimes 'tough love' comes into play, and families, friends, partners don't hold back but just tell you how it is. Sometimes this brutal truth works; other times, it pushes you further away and further down. That's when we start to hurt the people that love us, we close the door to the outside world and become alone. Every day becomes more negative and darker as time passes by.

Until YOU decide that enough is enough!

Something or someone will cause a reaction in your life and it will be enough for you to say: NO MORE! I have said this sentence so many times to different people and you can see in their eyes the disbelief that this could happen to them.

Imagine waking up one day and your outlook on life is suddenly different. Imagine that the moment your feet hit the ground you have changed your path of life, just because you said to yourself the night before, 'Tomorrow I want to be better; tomorrow I fight for a better life; tomorrow I will work to make my dreams come true.'

Changing a path *can* happen suddenly. Trust me, I know. I lost everything – my marriage; my home; life as I knew it went up in a puff of smoke. And I did what most people do, I became angry. I blamed everyone else, but not myself. I felt alone for the very first time in my life, and just like that my life went from light, happy, and positive to dark, negative, and with no sight of hope. I was in the gutter and I had lost everything that mattered.

But was I alone? Did I lose everything? How dark was my life? These were not questions I asked myself. But these were questions that a stranger I met in a bar one night asked me. I was doing my usual speech about how life was crap blah, blah, blah, but his eyes were different. He didn't share my views. He simply replied, 'You talk a lot of crap, you know that?' And then he hit me with it, 'Are you alone? Did you lose everything? How bad is your life? You are still healthy, and you are still here to tell the tale.'

Sad thing is, I don't even know this man's name. We just happened to be talking in a local bar where I found myself drinking in most nights. But amazingly, I walked out that bar that night, and the things he said to me went round and round my head.

And this was my turning point. This was the moment when a strange man in a little Spanish bar would open my eyes like never before. I decided that night that things had to change, and I went to bed with the mindset that tomorrow would be better. Nothing more... but just better.

Why am I telling you this? Because I want you to know that I learned from life. I want to share my story with you to make you aware that life will kick you down very quickly, but that you can turn it around just as quickly.

Life has plenty of paths and this means we can change direction whenever we want. We don't need to wait; we don't need someone to hold us there; we just simply flick that switch and decide that enough is enough.

*'THE POWER OF THE MIND IS CAPABLE OF SHINING THE LIGHT ON ANY DARK MOMENT.'*

*Salvatore Bruno*

Sometimes paths will cross with others just to confirm that we are on the right one. And the best path for you may not turn out to be the smoothest one. It may have lots of ups and downs, but if the light at the end is bright, the rewards are what you want, and you have plenty of fun along the way, then you are on the right path.

If this doesn't sound like your current path, then it's time for a change.

### Question:

*Are you ready to become a better version of you and choose a new path?*

# Chapter 4

# MIND OVER MATTER!

This is where I lose most folk. So many people I have met over the years fail to understand the simple motion of 'Mind over Matter' and why things happen to them.

Life is always going to be like that; nothing changes; bad things always happen to me. If you think like this, then guess what? You're right, nothing will ever change.

So many people believe that you have to be some sort of monk or ninja to be able to control your mind, to focus on thinking positive and using negativity to make you stronger.

But I am neither of those (even though, as a child, I always pretended to be a ninja – that's another story).

People CAN change they mindset, and this is happening every day, all around us. And guess what? These people are not monks or ninjas either.

People say to me, 'Tell me when this has happened.' Or they want facts to back up my statement. So I say the same as I always do:

I wasn't happy with the way my life was and the way it was going, so one day I decided to stand up and make a change. I wanted to be better, I wanted to learn, and I wanted my dreams to come true. Was it that simple? In one way, yes. I was down and in a dark place, so my only way was up.

I had choices, like everyone else. Stay the same, or change. I decided to go for the harder option – CHANGE!

Am I the only person who has done this? Hell, no. Thousands of people, maybe even millions, are doing this every single day. For some, it takes longer than for others, as everyone is different and no one person is at the same time and place than another person. We are all unique, and that's the amazing thing. We are all different, but we all have this inner strength to change our lives; we all have that internal switch, and we all have the power to flick that switch.

You may still be thinking that because you don't see it, it can't be true. Perhaps you only see people who are negative or positive, but you haven't seen that negative person fall and get back up, or the positive person who once was down and had nowhere to turn.

If you still don't believe me, that's fine. But let me give you some more facts; some proof, you could say.

Have you heard stories of men and women who have done things that they were told were impossible? I am not talking about magic; I am talking about those people who perhaps have been told by the doctors that they will never walk again, yet months later they take those first steps. How do they do it? With a super strong mindset and the determination to get the job done. And they have achieved it because these people told themselves, 'I will improve. I will be better. I will walk again.'

Imagine what that person must have felt when they were told they would never walk again. How would you cope if you were told that? Imagine the inner strength and mindset needed to overcome such a battle. Waking up every day and still unable to walk. And then one day... you make that small tiny step. And it's that small tiny step that will change that person's life forever.

Of course, that is an extreme example, but we all hear these amazing stories. I love to learn about someone who has had to overcome such a huge thing like that – the person who battled against illness like cancer and won; the person whose kidneys were failing and refused to let life stick him on a dialysis machine; those people who lost everything in a storm but still manage to see the fun in life; the ones who battle demons every day, but show the world that they will enjoy this life as much as anyone else; or the ones that are just not happy with something in life, a job, a relationship, and decide to make changes, even though sometimes the easiest things can be the hardest to overcome and change.

I am lucky and honoured to know such an amazing human – actually, a person very close to me, my brother in-law, Christopher Yianni. Back in January 2013, he had a kidney transplant. After a very successful operation, he could have decided to live life carefully and just go with the flow. But instead, he decided to view it as a second chance to live life to the max, and since that day he has made his dreams come true, living each day towards another dream, another memory. He travels around the world seeing amazing places and making epic memories with my sister. They live life as if it's a gift, and understand that dreams do come true.

One of Chris's dreams was to become a pilot. So he spent hours studying and finally, after doing all the tests and flight hours, he passed his exam. Now he takes to the skies as one of his amazing hobbies/loves.

I have been up there with him and, trust me, it's amazing to go up in a small 2- or 4-seater plane. You feel so connected with the skies. The first time

I sat in the passenger seat, I watched him prep the plane for take-off, and he was no longer my brother in-law but a pilot. Within moments, we started to move and were heading down the runway, then he pulled back and we started to lift. All of a sudden we were flying.

I was sitting in a plane that my brother in-law was flying, and it felt so surreal. I was so proud of him. And at that moment, when I looked at him, I understood why he does this. His eyes were wide open and he was enjoying the flight just as much as I was, because every time he takes to the skies it reminds him of how far he has come and what he has overcome.

We looked out and could see for miles. The sun was shining, and I was sitting there, thinking about nothing, my mind stunned by what my eyes were seeing. This is why, in my eyes, Chris is one of those legends. He went from the dark part of life

and turned it round to having a life that he 100%
enjoys, making a life which was a huge negative
and making it a hugely positive one. He is truly
living life his way, or should I say, my sister's way.
(Family joke! If you know Linda, you will
understand, ha ha.)

So, this is why it all depends on who you are,
how strong you can be, and at what point you say
to yourself, 'Enough is enough. I deserve better.'

*'IT'S SO IMPORTANT TO TAKE A
MOMENT SO YOU CAN TELL
YOURSELF YOU ARE WORTH IT AND
YOU CAN DO THIS.'*

*Salvatore Bruno*

I truly take my hat off to everyone who has had to
dig deep and change their mindset to overcome a
negative in their lives, no matter how big or small
the things were. Well done. I have so much respect
to you.

I have met some amazing people who have overcome such great things, and hearing their stories fills me with so much joy as you can feel the positivity flowing through their voice, you can see it in their eyes, and you can even feel it in the air.

You know what I am talking about. That person who makes you feel great when they talk to you; the ones who tell you a story, and your hairs stand on end and you feel alive. These legends have stories that I will never get bored of hearing, and they motivate me to do even better and continue to share their tales with others.

If you have an amazing story you want to share, please get in touch with me. I'd love to hear it.

So, the real questions are: how do you use your mindset to overcome the negatives in your life? How do you use it to change your life's path?

I didn't invent this, and I don't claim to have re-invented the wheel. I found out, like most people do, by just getting to that point where enough is enough and deciding to do something about it. It was only after I looked back that I realised what I had done

The difference is that I want to talk about it so that I can tell other people out there that they are not alone, and that they can do it, too. It doesn't matter how small or big the problem may be. You might not even know that the problem is, you just want to have a better life. You maybe hate your job, or can't stop thinking negatively about life. Or you're fighting a huge illness. But whatever your situation, you can use your mind to make things better.

*'TAKE CONTROL AND*
*START SAYING* **NO** *TO THE*
*NEGATIVITY AND* **YES** *TO POSITIVITY.'*
*Salvatore Bruno*

What would you change? What makes you unhappy on your journey through life? Do you feel too old to change? We can all improve our lives, no matter your age or background.

- Are you going to fail if you change your path? Quite possibly.
- Will it be hard? Yes.
- Will it be worth it? HELL, YES!!

I worked in a job were my boss was a complete dick, and every day I grew more and more negative, taking my anger out on my friends and loved ones. You've no doubt heard people at work saying, 'Don't bring your problems to work.' Well, it works both ways, and I am saying, 'Don't take your work problems home.'

If your work life makes you so upset or angry, you might take those feelings home and then unleash them on your partners, parents, kids, friends – the people who care about you.

The problem is that most of the time, people don't even realise it's them who are the problem – not the boss or work colleagues. Yes, these people you work with might be hugely annoying, but YOU are the one letting them get to you.

How many times have you heard, 'If you don't like your job, change it'? Yet you are the one making the excuses why not to change. So, one year passes, then another four, and seven years pass but nothing has changed, you are still not happy. I wonder why!

Guess what? YOU ARE THE PROBLEM, NOT YOUR WORKPLACE, BOSS, OR COLLEAGUES!

You know how long it took me to learn that? Too long.

The question is: are you the same as I was, and lying to yourself and blaming others when the real problem is you?

And this isn't just about your job. Perhaps you are not happy with your relationship. Your partner doesn't treat you well, hits you, mentally breaks you down, or you are just going out with someone because you don't want to be alone. Or the other thing I hear a lot, 'I always pick the wrong type of partners.'

Guess what? YOU ARE THE PROBLEM,

Yep, that's right. Your partner that is horrible to you, the one that mentally breaks you down or is just the wrong type in your life – you allow them to be there.

If you are reading this and recognise your own situation, don't worry! You are never alone, and you do have the strength to come out the other side. But for you to do that, you need to stand up and say, 'Enough is enough. I am better than this, and I deserve better.'

There are so many different reasons why people are not happy, but there is only one way to fix them. And that is to use your inner power and start using the gift that you were born with. It's been with you forever, and is ready to use whenever you want.

So, now is the time to improve, to become the better version of you. It's time to unleash the power and let your mindset take you on a new brighter path of life.

### Question:

*If you could snap your fingers and change your life, what would you want to change?*
*And why?*

# Chapter 5

# BREAKING THE MOULD!

It's amazing when you finally come to terms with the reasons why things are not going right, or why things are not how they are supposed to be. Finally accepting that you are to blame and that it's you that needs to adapt and change your path. When you realise that, it feels like a huge weight has been lifted. But, be warned. You will also feel a little lost, because for the first time in your life you are seeing things for what they are and the unknown can be a scary place. It can also be an exciting one!

Now that you are no longer blaming others, you understand that you are where you are due to the choices you made or did not make. So now you are standing on your own two feet, and you know that you control your journey and the path you walk down. You are the one that has got you to where you are now, perhaps due to a combination of different paths and events. But now you stand here, in this place, at this moment... and for the first time you understand what it feels like to live for the moment, to feel alive for this very moment in time – one that will never come again.

Your eyes are wide open but you are not sure which direction to take. Your options feel limitless and you feel overwhelmed, but you now understand that you can do anything you want.

Then something else happens at this moment – something that no-one will prepare you for, and it will hit you hard. Fear! Fear will show its face, and it will try and pull you back down the same path you were on because it's the one you know and are familiar with, and most people fear the unknown.

Why does fear show its face now? Simply because we are comfortable when we know what we are doing, when we have a routine, when life is easy, and when it's the same every day. But the moment we step out of our comfort zone and break the mould, that is when fear will show its face to scare us back into that safe place.

But not this time.

This time, we stand up and face it head-on.

*'EVERYTHING YOU EVER WANTED IS ON THE OTHER SIDE OF FEAR. THE PLACE WHERE DREAMS ARE MADE.'*
*George Addair*

Think of it like this. How many times have you heard people say, 'I don't like change'? Well, change is good. Especially when the path you are on is flat, negative, offers no enjoyment, and – worse – it makes you sad as it breaks you down bit by bit.

I never said that becoming a better version of you was going to be easy. I never said that it would happen overnight, or even at the first attempt, but it will be worth it when you make that change.

Focus on working hard and you can achieve anything you want. Imagine the world is yours and that any of life's paths are ready for you to try, there for your choosing. For the first time in your life, you have the choice to truly be happy within yourself, truly living life to the max, by finally connecting the dots and realising that any path of life is yours.

To stay positive, we must brace ourselves for the hard days that will come – and they will come. So, we prepare for the days when our paths will cross with a negative one, and we will be ready because we understand that life will have its ups and downs. When you know it's coming, it doesn't hit you as hard; it's like you are ready for the kick and are braced for impact, so when it does hit, you shrug it off and continue down your chosen path once again.

How do we get started then?

Your first step is admitting that you are to blame and to break the mould. Trust me, this is no easy feat, and it will take a lot of guts and determination. We humans are not programmed to take blame well and we all act in different ways. You will find that telling yourself you're not happy in life because of decisions you have made does not normally go down well. But once you have done that and actually believe it, then you are ready to take the first and most important step to a new and brighter future.

'THE FIRST STEP IN THE RIGHT
DIRECTION IS ALWAYS THE HARDEST.'
*Salvatore Bruno*

Before we go any further, we need to have a discussion about what we want. It can be a new job, to get out of your current relationship, or to make that first step to walking again. Whatever the reason, it will be the outcome of you breaking the mould and making that first step.

And here come some HARD home truths. Unfortunately that first step has been known to make people fall flat on their faces, or for a door to close just as they get near it. But all this is part of the learning curve, and it will make you stronger and more determined to continue and succeed. The great thing is that once you have decided to improve and become a better you, there is no real going back. Only the weak will return to a path and a life in which they know they weren't happy.

If you fall, you must get up; if a door closes on you, then you must look for another one. Or as I prefer to look at it, to KICK THE DOOR IN. You may say that sounds a bit harsh, but just wait until you feel so determined that you won't let any close door stop you, that no wall is too thick, and no mountain too high.

I remember reading a quote years ago from the legendary basketball player Michael Jordan, when he said: 'Obstacles **don't have** to stop you. If you **run** into a **wall, don't** turn **around** and give up. Figure out how to climb it, go **through** it, or work **around** it.'

Whatever way you decide to look at it, you will not turn back, and you will not go back to where you came from. It's at this time that your mindset will grow and give you the strength to carry on.

So, now you have made that first step and understand the challenges you face towards breaking the mould of your life.

You have decided to be better, you have decided that you want a better life, and you now know it starts with one simple but important first step.

It's time for you to grow as a person, and now anything is possible!

Life is all about choices, and yes, we all make some wrong ones. But if you have been making loads of wrong ones and then you see your mistakes, surely things can only get better. Right? Why wait to change your life when you can do it now, and truly start to walk down a path that you deserve, a path filled with whatever positives you desire?

We truly only have one life. So, isn't it worth breaking that mould and taking that first step? Doesn't it sound worth it? Doesn't it sound like a path of life which will be brighter than the one you have now?

Imagine if you broke your mould, changed your routine, and choose a different path – one with endless limitations, a path where your dreams could become a reality. Sounds too good to be true?

Well, to most it is. To most people, what I am talking about is far too hard to attempt, or they are already too scared to take that first step. Fear has already beaten them.

This is why not everyone is living the life they want. It's there for the taking if you want it, but you MUST want it and you MUST be willing to put the hard work in.

If you are willing to stop blaming others, then come and join me on a journey that will change your outlook on life forever. The world is a big enough place for us all to enjoy our dreams, so if you are ready then let's not wait any longer. Let's take the first step to a new you, a stronger you, and the path to your new exciting life.

### Question:
*What reason would stop you breaking the mould and start walking down a new positive path of life?*

# Chapter 6

# FIRST STEP!

The first, most powerful moment of your new life is the moment when you decide to make that initial step to the new improved you – the first step down a new path.

Will it be difficult?

Will it have its ups and downs?

Will it push you to your limits?

Yes to all, but most of all will it be worth it? Well, that is for you to answer.

The time to break the mould and make your first step is now. So, the real questions are:

Which direction do you want to step towards?

What do you want to change about you or the life you are living?

What are the things in your life that would make a huge change if removed or changed?

Let's try this out right now. Let's see if you really have what it takes. If I stood in front of you now and asked you straight out, would you be able to give me 4 things in your life you would change and why? Do you already know what you would say? If you don't know, have a real deep think about that one. 4 things!

Once you have done this, it will give you a better understanding of what needs to be done. Sometimes the answers are not nice to come to terms with. Some are easier than others to change, but either way, these things must change in your life for you to improve. Some people will tell you that making these changes will be easy, but I am here to tell you otherwise. It will be hard, and your first step could cause you to take 3 steps back at first, but you must keep going. Remember the quote from Michael Jordan; trust me it will all be worth it.

It doesn't matter what your background, what age you are, or your gender, you are unique. And you were given a gift when you were born, and that gift was LIFE.

*'THE GREATEST GIFT YOU WILL EVER HAVE IS THE GIFT OF LIFE. APPRECIATE IT.'*

*Salvatore Bruno*

Just because you may have been walking down a path that was chosen for you, or one that you just ended up on, it doesn't mean you have to stay on it. These paths of life can be changed at any time.

For example, you wake up one morning and you find out you have an illness, someone close to you has died, you lost your job, or your partner that you dearly love is leaving you. Any one of these will push you off your path of life, and without any choice you find yourself going along a path that you do not like nor want.

On the other side of the coin, your path can also change in a positive way. For example, someone close to you has recovered from an illness, you have been promoted, or you meet someone who loves and cares for you. All these things can change your life in a blink of an eye – it can be that quick!

The real power is controlling when you make the step from one path to another, and improving your life one step at a time.

Have you ever heard the quote, 'Where one door closes, another opens'? I truly believe this. But if you don't, then when a door closes you won't be looking for the other door, as you will be too focused on the closed door.

This is when your negative eyes are going to make you miss opportunities, and without even realising you find yourself slowly falling down into a dark place once again. But people who have broken the mould see life with positive eyes, so when that door closes they are already focusing on where the next door maybe, waiting to catch the open door – and, of course, they always do.

*'SOMETIMES THINGS NEED TO FALL*
*APART SO BETTER THINGS CAN FALL*
*TOGETHER.'*
*Marilyn Monroe*

This is why you will hear stories from other people about how they left a job they hated, but start their new job on the following Monday. Or they finally left the really horrible boyfriend/girlfriend, only to bump into a really nice person at the bus stop. I could write a long list of different examples, but you understand what I mean. Opportunities will happen to people who look for them, who chase them, who want them.

Another problem with taking that first step is that too many people put a huge amounts of pressure on themselves by putting a 10-year, a 5-year or even a 6-month plan in place but have no idea how to get started. So, this means the pressure starts to build from day one.

Essentially, that means giving yourself an impossible task, with failure being inevitable. Wouldn't it be better to come up with a plan, then break that plan into smaller steps, knowing what each step was, and thus allowing you to make the first step a lot easier because you already know what other steps are to follow. Don't get me wrong.

I 100% agree life plans are good, but not if you can't plan them in small steps. There is no point in setting yourself up for failure, so plan well.

Life doesn't have to be difficult. It is up to you to change those negative things in your life and make them positive. Use the negatives to build up the strength to change your life and take that first important step. Millions of people every single day are doing this and improving their lives, so don't be left behind! You deserve to take control and start that new journey to becoming a new, improved you.

The first step is never your last; it's simply a small step in a different direction. It's not like I'm asking you to take a massive jump, so why fear such a small step? Overcoming any issues or problems is hard, but next time you are faced with a negative in your life, think: Which small step could get me away from this situation? Which path could I take to avoid this happening again? Sometimes we focus on the first step so much that we forget the bigger picture.

Always remember that you are taking these steps to get closer to your dreams, to a happier and more positive life, to becoming the best versions of yourself, if these steps in your eyes are not worth taking, my question to you is: Do you really value your life enough?

Surely, taking that small step in the right direction is worth it if your dreams are at the end of that path?

It's your choice. It's only one step, followed by other little steps. Simple!

### *Question:*

*Do you truly believe that you are destined for a certain life, or do you believe that you have the power to change it?*

# Chapter 7

# WHO ARE YOU?

Now that you have decided to take that first step on your new path of life, there is another important issue you have to tackle. It probably sounds very strange, but my next question to you is: Have you ever really asked yourself who are you?

It's a question you will be asked throughout your life at different times – at school, out and about, at a job, in an argument. You would have seen it in films, and the actor always has a cool line to describe who he or she is.

Who are you? *I AM BATMAN!*

Who are you? *I AM WONDER WOMAN!*

Who are you? *JAMES. JAMES BOND!*

Who are you? YOUR WORST NIGHTMARE!

I'm sure you get what I mean. But really, 'who are you?' goes a lot deeper than that. It's you as a person; it's you as a whole package. This planet is big, and there is plenty of space for you to be anything you want. So, have you thought about who you are or who you want to be?

Of course, it's a different story if you ask a child this question. From a child, you will get some amazing answers. Not because they are trying to be smart, but because they believe in what they're saying. As a child, you have no fears; you let your imagination run free, and you don't see things through negative eyes. As a child, you can be anything you want.

But as we grow up, our imagination is pushed to the back of our minds and fear kicks in more and more. We can't pretend to fly any more as an adult. It's silly, right? Or is it? I have two very good friends who loved the idea of flying as kids, and even as adults are still doing it regularly.

One does parachuting, and the other flies with his wingsuits. (If you don't know what that is, look it up; it is as close to flying as you will get.) And as I mentioned earlier in the book, my brother-law Chris flies planes.

Now let's think about a kid that played with cars, making roaring sounds as the vehicles raced around on the carpet. Years later, that same person is speeding down a straight on one of the most famous tracks in the world, throwing their race car into the bend at incredible speed, the adrenaline making them push to drive faster and to win. This is no longer that kid that was playing cars on his parents' floor; this is now an adult doing what they love. Ask them as a kid who they are, and they'll reply, 'I am a racing car driver.' Ask them now as an adult, and the answer will be the same.

What were the things you did as a child that you thought you would grow up to be? Now the idea of me asking 'Who are you?' could open the doors to so many different answers.

Imagine if you could leave the job you hate, to go and do something you love. Imagine if you could be the person you always wanted to be, but because of your negative thoughts and fear holding you back you pushed that idea to the back of your mind.

Well, now I am telling you it's time. Time for you to open up that imagination and be whatever you want. You already know fear will show its face, but you will be ready. So it's time we flick that switch from negative to positive and let your imagination run wild.

And it's never too late. I know older people who have left a job to become self-employed in a bid to chase their dreams, and we've all heard of people quitting their work to go off and travel to far-off places, or person who grew up as a boy but finally admits they always wanted to be a girl.

So, I will ask you again: if you had no fear and you could let your imagination run wild, how would you answer if I asked you, 'Who are you?'

> *'TO KNOW WHO YOU ARE,*
> *YOU NEED TO FORGET WHAT*
> *PEOPLE TOLD YOU TO BE.'*
>
> *Unknown*

You see, it's not about who you were; it's about who you want to be. So many people around us are taking that first step on the new path of life, and now you can be one of them. This is about you being the happiest you have ever been, doing things you deeply love, and surrounding yourself with positive people and making amazing memories.

This is about you grabbing life with both hands and making it anything you want. It took me a long time to understand this part, for the simple reason that no-one explained it to me. No-one showed me the way; no-one showed me how easy it could be to change my life from a negative to a positive.

I had to find out the hard way, but now I am telling you that it is easy. It's as simple as one step here and another step there, and the best part of all if that the only person preventing you from doing this, is you.

So, don't hold yourself back. It's time for you to be whoever you want to be.

### Question:

*What do you miss about your imagination*
*fun as a child?*

# Chapter 8

# I AM SUPERHUMAN!

I love this bit. When I say it, people look at me like I am mad, but... I AM SUPERHUMAN!

That word has so many different meanings. Have you ever looked at someone and thought that they were superhuman? Do you think *you* are? What is *your* special power?

I truly believe it all depends on the moment or the person, and most of all the reason.

You are probably wondering what on earth I am going on about, but I am going to tell you how to take your mindset to a whole new level, and how to join the world of superhumans. Trust me, this is no film; this is real life. And before you ask, yes, I believe I am superhuman. And my super power is that I believe that you can achieve anything. Nothing is impossible.

I wasn't always like this, as you now know. But certain things happened in my life to push me down a path that would, years later, open my eyes fully. And now I stand here with this power.

Do I believe that I am a superhuman? Simple answer: Yes.

Sounds crazy, right? I don't blame you for thinking I have lost my marbles, but hear me out. Do you ever hear of someone doing something unbelievable, and you've thought to yourself, 'How the hell did he/she do that?'

Well, this is where the magic happens. This is how you become a superhuman. The way I look at it, a superhuman is not someone who wears a cape and flies through the sky, or can turn into a really strong green man. No. A superhuman is someone that does something that makes people stop and stare, makes people say, 'Wow!', as they cannot believe what they have witnessed. I believe we see superhumans every day, but some of our minds are more closed off so can't see them.

You are probably sitting there now saying, 'Go on then, give me an example.' Okay, here are just a few.

Did you know that just before May 1962, Jack Kirby witnessed a woman lifting a car to save her trapped baby, which then inspired him to create the character The Hulk?

In 1984, Jack LaLanne ('the first fitness superhero'), became famous for towing 70 rowboats with passengers from Queen's Way Bridge to the ship *Queen Mary* in the USA, while shackled, handcuffed, and fighting winds and a strong current. He was already 70 years old at the time.

But for me a more recent event which made me go 'Wow!' was from a superhuman I am honoured to know. His name is Ross Edgley, and if you don't know who this man is, you will look him up after I tell you. He has completed plenty of unbelievable challenges, but the last one took the world by storm, proving that superhumans do exist. His challenge, which also made history, was swimming around the UK – the whole of the United Kingdom! – and it took 157 days of swimming 12 hours each day for him to complete the 1,791 mile (2,864kms) journey. Thousands of people watched every day as he battled to make his way around the country.

So many people doubted him. But in November 2018, as he walked up the shoreline to the finish line in Margate, he became the first person in history to do this incredible swim and made so many people truly wonder how it had been possible.

I look up to people like Ross. When I see people like him achieve amazing things like this, it makes me feel like I can do anything, that nothing is impossible.

But these are the superhumans that stand out from the crowd. What about the ones we don't see? The firemen who ran back into a house to save someone, the surgeons that carry out incredible operations, the lifeguard that jumped into the sea to save someone from certain death. I'm certain that I have missed out loads of different types of superhumans. But if you know of one, I would love to hear all about it, as these stories fill me with huge joy and warmth.

# 'SUPER HUMANS DON'T NEED CAPES, AS THEIR MINDSET IS THE TRUE SUPERPOWER.'

*Salvatore Bruno*

The truth is that each day you could be walking past or sitting next to a superhuman and not even know it. These superhumans are everywhere. They look like a normal human, but inside they are different. They have a story, and if they told you, you would no doubt be wowed by it.

And there is no reason why you can't join them. But be warned: it takes time; it takes a huge amount of guts, motivation, and determination. And most of all, your mindset must be strong. You can't doubt yourself. But if you do, you have to shrug that off and continue to get the job done. There is no room for negativity in the world of superhumans.

If I stood in front of you and said that I believe in you and that you can everything we have talked about so far in this book, would you be willing to take that first step? To take that step onto a new path that will lead you to believe that anything is possible? The simple fact is: YOU CAN. And the only person who can stop you is YOU.

So, don't be left behind. Tell yourself that you want to be a superhuman, and you want to make the impossible possible. That's when those hurdles in your life that previously looked like mountains now look like molehills; the obstacles that felt like huge walls which would stop you being happy with life, now seem like doors onto a new path. Everything looks different through positive eyes. With the mindset of a superhuman, things suddenly don't seem so bad, life doesn't look so grey, and you can see solutions instead of problems.

It's your choice. You either want to change, or you don't; it's that simple. Think hard about it.

What decision would you make?

No-one will ever be able to help you make that step. People like me can only show you and guide you. Then it's up to you to build up the courage to cross over to the positive side. We are all here waiting for you!

### *Question:*

*What excuse would you give yourself for not wanting to become the best version of yourself, to become a superhuman?*

# Chapter 9

# PREPARING FOR
# THE PUSH BACK!

It is all very well me sitting here writing this book from my terrace with a cup of tea beside me as I look onto the beautiful views, the sun beaming in the sky, and listening to *Two Steps From Hell*. Life feels great. My life is going down a path that I am enjoying.

But most of all, I am in control. And the one thing I am always prepared for now is the PUSH BACK. This is something that you will see happen a lot. It can come from the people you know or strangers. Sometimes you won't see it coming, other times you will see it coming from a mile away. Or you will wake up and, bang! it's there.

But we must always prepare ourselves for the PUSH BACK.

What is it? It is something I made up to help me focus on the negatives that come my way in life – and they do. Life is not always blue skies and sunshine, and anyone who is living a positive life and is truly honest will admit that those dark days do come.

So, I came up with the term PUSH BACK. It is when someone or something is trying to push you back to the negative side, but also when a force of negativity is coming down on you and you need to PUSH BACK.

So, these two words can have two very different meanings:

**PUSH BACK** – When someone or something is pushing you back to the negative side.

Or

**PUSH BACK** – When you need to fight fire with fire, push back and stand your ground, be clear that you won't go back. The positive side is where you belong, so you have to push back.

I realised very early on that something or someone will always try and ruin your path. That's life. People get jealous that you are happy or doing well for yourself. Life will suddenly throw a spanner in the works for whatever reason, but the difference is that when you are prepared for it you deal with it much better.

It's like the boxer who knows the punches are coming. Imagine if you had a fighter who could be one step in front of his opponent, who knew when the punches were coming and from what direction, as though his opponent was in slow motion. That would be a great gift, right?

Well, this is how we must prepare for the path ahead. For you to be truly happy and to achieve the life you want, you must understand that someone or something will try and ruin it. But understanding the push back will allow you to prepare, to deal with, and most of all to OVERCOME the push back, whatever it may be.

I want you to think back to a time when a push back has happened to you. Think of why it happened. Was it a person or thing that caused it? Then I want you to think about how you would deal with the same situation now, if you knew you could push back.

*'YOU MAY NOT CONTROL*

*ALL THE EVENTS THAT ARE COMING,*

*BUT YOU CAN DECIDE*

*HOW YOU DEAL WITH THEM.'*

*Salvatore Bruno*

I must state that when I say 'push back', I don't mean to physically push someone. I don't want you getting charged with assault (I just wanted to make that clear). Push back is all mental; it's all done within your head; it's all about controlling your emotions and overcoming the negativity that is thrown at you. So we call this a 'mental push back'.

The fact is that it takes time to get used to this. There will be days where you think you are prepared, but something goes wrong, it throws you off, you didn't push back, and whatever it was that has pushed you has made you sad, upset, angry or, even worse, started to take you down a path you do not want to be on.

Don't panic! I have made some rules that have helped me and clients in the past to overcome these push backs, and I still use these rules today.

**Rule 1:** DO NOT PANIC. If you panic, it will be hard for you to deal with the situation in a controlled manner.

**Rule 2:** STOP what you are doing and take a TIME OUT. Remove yourself from the situation, go for a walk, into a quiet room, listen to music/podcast, something to stop you thinking about the moment and the situation.

**Rule 3:** UNDERSTAND and accept that what has happened is negative and is a push back. Accepting it will allow you to deal with the situation better, and let your emotions calm, allowing you to focus.

**Rule 4:** SEE the push back for what it is. You will see it differently now that you are calm and back to the correct mindset, observing life through those positive eyes.

**Rule 5:** PUSH BACK! You have taken time, you have prepared, and now you are ready to do your push back to get back to the path you chose. This rule is hard and, to be honest, could take a few attempts. Don't worry, though. You are focused, so you will overcome.

**Rule 6:** REMEMBER what you have achieved and overcome. This will make you stronger, and will prove to you that you are focused, determined, and truly want this positive and happy life.

Using these rules will be hard the first time. But once you have used them and overcome the push back, you will learn from it, you will improve, and you will adapt, making you stronger than before.

It's a simple fact that we need these negative push backs to allow us to grow and make us stronger. If we didn't have them, we wouldn't have any need to improve so would just stay the same. And we all know that staying the same will lead you nowhere.

Now you know that your new path of life will have its negative moments along the way, but by using the push back rules you know how to overcome and get back to your positive and happy state.

I would love to say to you that life is plain sailing and that there is never a cloud in the sky, but I would be lying. I would rather prepare you for how things are, and make you aware of what life has to offer – good and bad.

That's why I don't hold back my punches. I stand up and say it how it is, because I have been there. I have learnt. I have adapted, and I am continuously improving. And that's why I am here writing this and showing you how you can overcome the push backs of life. The only thing you have to do is to be willing to learn, adapt, and improve.

**Question:**

*Are you ready to improve, adapt, and learn?*

# Chapter 10

# NEVER UNDER-ESTIMATE
# YOUR INNER POWER!

The power of you is another subject I talk a lot about. And this can involve different outlooks. You can look at it physically or mentally to get a better understanding of it, but both are as important as each other.

We are all born with this inner power built into us, like a muscle. And as you start to grow from birth, so does this inner power. Unfortunately, with most people it is pushed deep inside and never really used. So, it's left there still growing, but at such a slow rate you never realise it's there.

I always use the example of it being like a muscle, because we all have muscles but some people train them more than others. On the ones who train and use them, the body looks different, takes on a new shape, and is growing and developing. But others can't see their muscles, and they are lying beneath the surface of the skin, hiding away from the outer world.

Well, this is just like your inner power. You just need to develop it, and after time you will see it and so will everyone else.

What is this inner power for? And why shouldn't we under-estimate it?

Imagine you had something inside you that would allow you to push past your limits, overcome things that you thought impossible, give you strength to push back, allow you to stay strong where others around you fall, and keep you motivated and determined when everything is going against you. Just imagine if you had this inner power to overcome all of the above, plus so much more. Well, actually, you do!

You just need to look deep and believe it. You see, I don't believe that motivation and determination come from others; they come from within. Perhaps you think that a song, speech, or podcast will pick you up, but what they do is trigger your inner power. Whatever the trigger is, it will fire up your internal furnace and allow your inner power to kick start. And, oh boy, once it starts, you feel alive!

And it's at that moment when you feel different, ready to take on anything, no mountain is too high, no challenge is too big, nothing is impossible to overcome... that's when problems turn into solutions. And that's why it's so important that we believe in it and, most of all, in ourselves. We do have the POWER; we CAN overcome anything; and we WILL become a better version of ourselves.

*'YOUR INNER STRENGTH IS*
*YOUR OUTER FOUNDATION.*
*IT'S TIME TO BUILD.'*
*Allan Rufus*

Over the years I have discovered that there are different types of coaches. You have the ones who truly know what motivation and support means, and you have the others who have no idea. And this is where I found out my clients could achieve amazing things if I could just change the way they looked at things.

Imagine I gave you a workout and nutrition plan but you had no motivation to do it, or – even worse – you didn't believe you could achieve your goal. What do you think would happen after 4 weeks, 8 weeks, or even 12 weeks? I will tell you. You'd feel worse than when you started, because not only would you look no different but you would also have failed to meet your goal.

The real question in that scenario is: who is to blame – the coach, or you? I believe the coach is to blame!

I must point out that I am talking about the clients who try but have failed, due to not having the correct support, the true motivation, and the determination they need.

Now imagine we do it differently. I give you the same plan, but this time we fire up that furnace, we make sure you feel alive, we remove the doubts of I CAN'T and replace them with I CAN.

We grab your inner power and turn it up like a volume control. We unleash that inner power like huge beams of lights from a lighthouse, so people can see it from miles away. You no longer walk with your head facing the floor. Your inner strength has made you believe in yourself, which means you are proud of who you are and, most of all, of what you can achieve. Now your inner power is awake, it's ready and, most importantly, so are you. And that then means no goal is too big, nothing is impossible, and you will achieve it.

One of my favourite quotes:

*'BELIEVE AND YOU WILL*
*ACHIEVE ANYTHING'*

*Salvatore Bruno*

Now you understand that if you are failing and you can't find things to motivate you, then you are looking at your situation wrong. Don't look for motivation. Look for those triggers, then let your inner power fire up, and watch as the motivation flows to smash those goals. And the more you do this, the bigger your inner power becomes... just like growing muscles.

You just need to believe you can, and NEVER under-estimate yourself and your true power. You are born to succeed; you are born to overcome; and you are born with an inner power that you can grow to make amazing things happen. So, make those dreams a reality, smash those goals, or simply just keep yourself on your positive and happy path.

Don't under-estimate your power. Embrace it and truly become the person you are destined to be.

*'IF OTHERS CAN BELIEVE IN YOU,*
*WHY CAN'T YOU BELIEVE IN*
*YOURSELF?'*
*Salvatore Bruno*

## *Question:*

*Are you truly ready to unleash your inner power? And what is the first thing you are going to use this power to overcome?*

# Chapter 11

# BECOMING THE BEST!

By now you should know that your new positive and happy life awaits you, you understand that you need to use your inner power to get you there, and your positive eyes are already seeing life differently. It is now time to make that decision to become better and become the best you can be. There is no more waiting needed. You are ready, and you have the tools and the power to achieve this. So, what now?

Well, now we plan. We plot out the direction in which you want to go, because without a definite direction you could end up walking around in circles, and we don't want that.

At this stage we need to really embrace your possibilities and what is out there for you. The world is yours for the taking, so what direction do you want to take? Have you already made that decision? Do you know what you want to achieve?

If you have, then you are 100% ready. But let's say you haven't. Let's say you don't know what you want. I want to make this as easy as possible for you, so that you can make that decision and take the next step onto your path of life.

So, if you could pick any life, if you could be anyone, who would that be, and why?

The reason I start with this is not because it's right to copy. But for someone who has been locked in a negative world for so long, it can be hard to make a new path. It could be difficult to adjust to making decisions. So don't worry and don't put any pressure on yourself. We can start slowly, and this is why I asked if you have ever looked at someone else's life and wished you could have a life like that. It might be someone you look up to, a famous person, or just an idea/dream. Whatever or whoever it is, let's work with it and come up with your way of getting there, because there is no point in copying someone else's steps or trying to be the same as someone else as we know that does not work. We need to find the right way for you.

## 'WE ARE SPECIAL AS WE ARE UNIQUE'
### Salvatore Bruno

Being unique is something that makes our journey even better and exciting. It will take us into the unknown, it will allow us to stand out, and it will allow us to stand tall and be proud just being us. Yet many people forget this.

Even the simple things can make such a difference. For example, imagine you are talking to your friend or work colleague and he or she is discussing this amazing film they watched last night and they say, 'OMG. It's the best film ever, you must watch it.' How many times have you had this conversation? So, you go away, you watch this so-called amazing film, and two hours later you ask yourself, *What the hell did I just watch?* You hated it.

But how is this possible? Your friend said it was the best film ever, but you just wasted two hours of your life.

Actually, it's simple – we are all different. Even the people we are connected to have certain things which are way off the mark and completely different with regard to things they like, etc. But you should see this is a gift, because if we were all the same, life would be boring, right? No-one would stand; no-one would be better than anyone else; no-one would help others, etc.

This is why you can have any life you want. You have everything you need: the tools; the mindset; and now you know you are unique. So even if you walked down the same path as someone else, you would end up doing and achieving different things.

Right, let's go back to making that decision on where you go from here. Which path do you want to choose? Where do you want to end up? Who do you want to be?

*'10 YEARS FROM NOW, MAKE SURE YOU CAN SAY THAT YOU CHOSE YOUR LIFE, NOT THAT YOU SETTLED FOR IT.'*

*Mandy Hale*

When I first started my journey, I didn't have any idea where I wanted to be or go. I just wanted to be happier, and that was enough for me to start walking down a new path, away from my negative life and the life I used to live, leaving the person I used to be behind. But I discovered that the more I walked down this path, the more I changed and the more I started seeing things differently.

Obviously, it didn't all happen overnight. It takes time, but the one thing I knew was that I was becoming better and I was heading down a better path – a path towards becoming a better version of me.

This is when you start to understand the power of taking control of your life. You find that the things that used to bother you no longer have any effect. You instead find yourself looking for the solution rather than focusing on the problem. And you fully understand that if you are not happy with the path you are on, you can simply change it for a better one.

Finally, you have control to be the real you, the person you want to be, and you can work towards making everything you ever dreamed about come true. The things you could do are limitless, and the world is there ready to be explored.

*'WHEN YOU NO LONGER FEAR LIFE AND BELIEVE IN YOURSELF, LIFE BECOMES LIMITLESS.'*
*Salvatore Bruno*

The world is there to be learned from and to be seen. And most important of all, you are ready to truly be alive – something that most people will never get to feel because they are held back by fear, not wanting to change, and happy to stay following others.

Not us, though. We are here to live our lives, to become the best we can, and to make sure we make all those dreams a reality. We will no longer stay in the shadows of others; it's time for other people to stand in our shadows! And it's time for us to do what we thought was impossible – to live a life full of colour, positivity, and one in which we are truly happy.

Becoming the best version of yourself is the only way you will continue to push for a better and happier life. It will keep you pressing forward and looking for those open doors when doors close in front of you.

- When you are continually trying to LEARN, you will.
- When you continually try to ADAPT, you will.
- When you continually try to IMPROVE, guess what? That's right, you will.

Learn, Adapt, and Improve. These three things will keep that inner fire alive, keep you looking for that next opportunity, keep you motivated and determined to become the better version of yourself, make for a truly enjoyable, positive, and amazing journey, and help you truly understand the person you are meant to be.

The time to believe in yourself is now. It's time for you to start the new journey on becoming the better version of you and to find out what you are truly capable of. Come on, the world is yours. Take it, enjoy it, and most of all, go and show the world who you are!

*'DON'T TELL PEOPLE WHO YOU ARE,*

*SHOW THEM'*

*Salvatore Bruno*

**Question:**

*Where is your first dream going to be taking you?*

# Chapter 12

# YOU ARE YOUR WORST ENEMY!

Sometimes when I am honest with someone, it hurts. I know it's not what that person wants to hear, but I do it because sometimes we need to hurt to overcome our hurdles in life, to conquer those mental battles which will happen over and over again. You see, I wasn't joking when I said your life journey will be filled with ups and downs, but the worst thing of all is that you will be the cause of most of it.

So I will always tell you the truth. The hard fact is that you are going to be your worst enemy; we humans can't help it. Even today it still happens to me. My mind plays games, something triggers those negative thoughts, and BANG, before I know it my mind goes into overdrive and all this doubt and fear comes into my mind, I start to worry about 'what if's' or 'that I won't succeed', etc – things that normally I do not even waste time thinking about. But it's there now, the seed of doubt, and you planted it there. If you don't get rid of it quickly, it will grow, and it won't stop until you stop it and snap out of it.

*'THE MOMENT YOU START TO DOUBT YOURSELF IS THE MOMENT YOUR INTERNAL BATTLE BEGINS.'*
*Salvatore Bruno*

The power of the mind is an amazing thing; I would even go as far as saying it's beautiful. And I say this because I have seen it, seen what it has done for me and for others. I have seen what some people have achieved with it, but with a flip of a coin I have seen it take people down and others not achieving things because they doubted themselves. To put it simply: you can have it all – you truly can have your cake and eat it – BUT it comes with a price.

The stronger you get, the easier it can be to doubt yourself, because your goals will become bigger and bigger and some will seem unreal. Even using the word unreal or labelling it a 'big goal' could put that doubt in your head. Or you hear of people trying to achieve something but they have failed, and immediately your own doubt starts. But you must never forget that as quickly as things changed, you can also flick that same coin and get back to achieving your dreams.

There will come a time when you start to overcome things – big things which might previously have been thought of as impossible

– and the more you overcome, the stronger your mindset becomes. Then BOOM, you start to unleash your inner strength and it's like a rocket flying through space at super speed. You are flying, nothing seems to be able to stop you, whatever someone says or throws at you just bounces off you. You have no doubts, no fear. You are UNSTOPPABLE!

*'BECOMING UPSTOPPABLE IS A MINDSET LEVEL THAT ONLY THE VERY STRONG-MINDED PEOPLE CAN ACHIEVE.'*

*Salvatore Bruno*

It's an amazing feeling to wake up with this kind of energy, this drive to succeed in life. It feels like every day is a gift and you enjoy every breath; every beam of sunlight is like a motivational message; the world and everything around you is fuelling your inner furnace; you walk around with a glow; your eyes tell people a story; you have joined the superhumans and truly understand the power you have, and it is endless.

This is why I am honest with you and with everyone I speak to about this matter, because life is too short to waste. Yes, there will be doubts and you will fear things, but imagine if we had no battles. Imagine if our goals were all easy to achieve. How good would you feel about achieving them?

This is why we humans will always be our worst enemies, for ourselves and others. We all know people who like to hurt others, who like to get into people's heads and make them doubt themselves or belittle those around them. There's the big boss who treats his staff like crap, the boyfriend who mentally attacks his partner that he supposedly loves, or the person at the bus stop who just likes to point out negative things about people, telling that woman she looks fat and shouting out 'four eyes' to the person next to them.

That's why it's easy to have doubts and fear things, because we will always read negative stories and hear things on the news that will make us doubt who we are and where we are going. We just can't get away from them, unless you live in a box – and that's not a good thing.

You must understand what your mind will do, as that will allow you to deal with what is to come, because even though we are our worst enemy, we are also superhumans that can achieve the impossible. Be prepared that you will spend time battling your mind's thoughts, sleepless nights, sadness, doubts, fears, and just all-round unhappiness; they have all to come. But I'll be honest, I wouldn't change it at all. I know that when we do have these battles, they make us stronger, drive us to be better, make us more determined, and teach us that we might be our own worst enemy but we are also our own saviour.

We can fight fire with fire, and our internal furnace will always be the greatest fire of them all. We have the power to overcome, because it's what we were born to do. We were born to walk on our own two feet, to finally choose our paths. As they get older, some will decide not to, but that's their choice and their loss. Not us. We have chosen, we have made our mind up, and we have not taken the easy route. We are going to walk through those battlegrounds with our head up high and come out the other side, stronger, fearless, and ready to face another day on our exciting journey of life.

*'YOU ARE YOUR WORST ENEMY!*
*WHICH MEANS NO-ONE ELSE CAN*
*DO ANY WORSE THAN WHAT YOU*
*CAN DO TO YOURSELF.'*
*Salvatore Bruno*

The battlegrounds are there in certain parts of your life path, but these battles are meant to grow you, to bring you down. And these battles will come and go, but the amazing thing is that with every battle you put out the fire on FEAR, on DOUBT, and you stand tall with your internal furnace roaring away, brighter than ever, hotter than ever, stronger than ever. With every battle you overcome, you truly become more and more unstoppable. You are becoming superhuman.

### Question:

*What is the thing you fear and*
*doubt the most?*

# Chapter 13

# YOUR WINNER CIRCLE!

Life is there for the taking. You now know that you are able, but how do you plan for it? How do you stop making too many mistakes?

Well, there is a game plan, a plan of action, and I call it the WINNER CIRCLE. It will keep you in check, on the right path, and it will also allow you to achieve your goals over and over again.

'So,' you ask, 'how does it work?'

Simple! We think first and then we take action. Imagine if you had no plan but you had the goal. You would know what you want but would have no idea how to get there and no clue what steps to take. As a result, that goal would feel a million miles away. However, if you planned it out, you would understand the steps to not only get there but how to achieve your goal.

Do you think the person who is going to climb Mount Everest just arrives at it one day and says, 'I am going to climb this today.'? Of course not. He plans it. He works towards the climb so that he knows how to overcome it.

And yes, I did use a very big mountain as an example, but that's the idea. Your goals and dreams need to be big, so you are going to have to work damn hard to achieve some amazing things, because that epic life you want won't come easily.

THE WINNER CIRCLE...

The first step to reaching the Winner Circle can be the hardest if you have no idea how to get there. But who wants an easy life, right? Below are the steps that will change your outlook on planning your goals and dreams forever:

## WINNER CIRCLE

**Step 1: Your Goal** – What you want to achieve, what you want to overcome. This could be anything. Some people call them goals, others targets or dreams. Call it what you want. It could be a dream holiday, the perfect job, weight loss, etc.

**Step 2: Plan** – Prepare to put your plan in place. What are the steps that you will need to achieve this. You might need to break the plan down into small steps if your goal is a really big one – as in Short-term, Mid-term, and Long-term goals. This step can take people months to make if the goal is huge. Others with smaller goals could come up quite quickly with a game plan.

**Step 3: Adapt** – Now you need to adapt your lifestyle to make sure you are heading in the right direction. You might need to add training sessions each day, if it is a fitness goal; you might need to start saving X amount of money each week, if your goal is a dream holiday. We are creatures of habit so adapting your life sounds easy but it can be difficult to put into place and to stick to. Use notes around your house as a daily reminder of why you need to stick to this new lifestyle. Use calendars so you know how far you have come and how far you have to go. Break old habits and adapt to your new routine, whatever it may be.

**Step 4: Achieve –** Go SMASH it, and don't stop until you have! This step could take you a while, and it could be one you have to do over and over again until you achieve your goal. Remember that not everyone achieves their goal at the first attempt, but that's not a negative. We have to put the hard work in to truly see the benefits of that work.

Some things will be easier to achieve, and there will be people who achieve things at the first attempt while it takes you two or three. Take, for example, the 17-year-old woman who is learning to drive. She has done all she can to prepare for the test, but she keeps failing due to nerves. She tries again – her third attempt. This time, she controls her nerves, does her test, and boom, the instructor tell her she has passed.

**Step 5: Success** – So many people bypass this step. DO NOT BYPASS THIS STEP!

It's so important for you to take time to appreciate what you have achieved, to enjoy your success, to take time to celebrate. If you don't, what is the point of putting in all that hard work and not tapping yourself on the back and saying WELL DONE!

I have always said, 'Success is success, however big or small the achievement is.' Please remember that. Not every goal will be a world record attempt, but it still needs to be celebrated. BE PROUD of what you have achieved, and ENJOY the moment.

**Step 6: Repeat** – You now know how to plan the steps to achieve any goal. You know what work is needed, the time it might take, you have planned it well, adapted to the plan, then went out there and achieved it. But you also took time to appreciate your success, so you know how good that feels. Now you can repeat it to achieve more goals, targets, and dreams – even bigger and better ones. So Step 6 is there to remind you to repeat the other steps and you will achieve your goals. So, back to Step 1 you go...

Now you have the steps of your WINNER CIRCLE, use them to achieve whatever your heart wants and make those dreams come to life. Anything is possible with the right plan, and you already know that your inner power will help you. With the correct mindset, you will battle those doubts and negative days, so what is stopping you?

I have seen people following these simple steps and achieve some amazing things in their personal and business life. Use it as you wish, and tell others or keep it as your magic key to achieving what you want.

All I want to do is show people that achieving some of the most amazing things in life can be as easy as following a few steps, overcoming the impossible by using the right mindset, and thereby making all your dreams come true and becoming the best version of you.

*'ACHIEVING SOMETHING HUGE CAN*
*BE DONE BY SIMPLY BREAKING IT*
*DOWN INTO SMALL STEPS.'*
*Salvatore Bruno*

So, what is going to be the first thing you are going to aim for?

Do you have more than one? If so, what are they?

What doubts do you have about your ability?

Do you believe you can achieve whatever you put your mind to? YES /NO

Okay. Do not go any further. Stop and truly think about these questions, get a pen and paper and write them out, then I want you to think really hard about your answers. By this stage of the book, you may already have some ideas, so think away and get those answers written down.

I want you to see your answers written down on paper in front of you, so that you can truly take them in. This will help you to understand how far you have come, or what you need to achieve.

However, you might feel you don't need to think about the answers and are confident in your ability. In that case, my superhuman friend, you are ready to plan and take those steps towards achieving your goals.

WELCOME TO YOUR WINNER CIRCLE!

*Question:*

*Out of all your goals, which scares you the most? And why?*

# Chapter 14
# AUTOPILOT!

It's truly amazing how we humans work, how our minds truly take over and we just go into autopilot. You start your day and the next minute you know it's lunchtime or, even worse, it's time for bed and you have no idea where the day went. Or you are driving to work and you are thinking about something, then next thing you are pulling up outside your office and can't remember the journey in. Or you are sitting on the train surrounded by people, but the moment you get off at your station, you can't remember what the people in front of you looked like.

You see, our mind is used to taking control and has done it for years. It was built into us from the moment we were born, and is the reason why people find themselves years down the line wondering where time has gone or, worse, what they have done. The mind's autopilot is there to guide us down the paths of life which we follow over and over again, the routes you take to work every single day, your daily routines, actions you take over and over again.

You can do it all these things with your eyes closed, right? That's because your mind has mapped it all out, knows what time you need to leave and how to get there, so the moment you leave your house, the moment those keys turn the ignition, we automatically activate our mind's autopilot without realising. The problem is, though, it sometimes doesn't stop with the journey to work, and continues throughout the day. So, some people have no idea that they are not living their lives at all; they are in constant autopilot and have no way of turning off the switch.

Have a think about how often your mind goes into autopilot and when. You might be surprised at the answers.

*'LIFE IS A SPECIAL JOURNEY AND A JOURNEY THAT YOU DON'T WANT TO MAKE ON AUTOPILOT.'*

*Salvatore Bruno*

Don't worry. You're not the only one this happens to. It sometimes happens to me, too, but not as often now because I like to control where I am going and to be in charge. Sometimes, though, it's nice to just go along for the ride, and it's easy.

I must admit, I did have it bad at one time. I used to work in an office, and my journey there took around an hour plus each way, down the famous M25. If you don't know that road, you're lucky, because it's famous for being like a car park with long queues of traffic and always busy. So I made a routine for myself that I would get up at 4.15am each day to miss all the morning traffic, and I even joined a gym near the office where I could train before starting work. This made for very long days, but you do what you have to, don't you?

One day I got to the gym, and one of my new-found exercise mates came up to me and said, 'You're early this morning.' I looked at him like he had two faces. 'What are you on about?' I replied. He said, 'It's 4:30am.'

I was a little shocked and couldn't understand what had happened? How could I have been unaware of the time?

I didn't know back then, but I had been in autopilot for nearly two years, getting up early, driving to the gym, doing my workout, and then driving to work. But on that day the difference was that I hadn't heard my alarm. I just got up, and next thing my mind had kick-started my routine, and before I knew it I was standing face-to-face with this friend in the gym at 4.30am, with no recollection of my drive in or anything.

So, I started to ask myself how long I had been in autopilot. And the real shock was that I had no idea. I couldn't recollect the last time I really remembered driving to the gym.

Realising this, I knew that something had to change; this wasn't right. I started to ask around to see if anyone was going through the same situation, and some people's faces were a picture of shock and surprise when I asked if they could remember their journey into work that day. So many of them realised that they had no idea. A few just lied so they didn't look stupid, because they thought I was trying to catch them out. But I wasn't. I was truly interested in how many of us this happened to, and surprised to discover that it was a very high percentage.

The next morning's drive to the gym was different. On that occasion, I watched every car, every road sign, really listening to the songs on the radio. When I actually got to the gym, everything felt different. I had got myself there with no autopilot.

*'HOW CAN YOU APPRECIATE THE WAY A CAR DRIVES IF YOU ARE BEING CHAUFFEURED?'*

*Salvatore Bruno*

I decided to take things a little further, and I looked at what I had gained by not going into autopilot.

The main thing was TIME – something we are always moaning we don't have enough of. Yet we are wasting minutes, hours, days, and even years, as we autopilot our life away. Well, not any more; not for me.

I decided that I was going to put that time to good use. But what could I do while driving for over two hours every day? (To be honest, it was closer to three hours, as the evening traffic was always bad.) So let's say around three hours of my day for five days a week. What could I do with those 15 hours I was suddenly giving myself back per week?

I wanted to improve myself, so listening to music wasn't enough. And reading a book while driving is very much against the law, so I was introduced to Audible and the world of eBooks and podcasts. Wow, wow, and more wow! That's all I am going to say.

Before that point I'd never really had time to read books – or maybe I didn't want to – but this just opened up a whole new door of learning for me. I had gained all this time which meant I could, in theory, give myself a target of listening to two books per month. And that's exactly what I did.

I looked up subjects I wanted to learn and understand more about, like mindset, nutrition, fitness, business, languages – the list was long. and from then on, there I was, every single day learning something new. There was no room for autopilot any more, as each day brought new words, a new chapter, more information for me to take in.

I was actually learning, and for the first time in my life I was enjoying books and taking everything I wanted from them. There was no-one around to bother me; it was just me, an open mind, and this time that I had gained each day.

I even took things one step further and listened to audiobooks when I was driving or travelling, and podcasts when I was doing my steps (daily walks).

Autopilot had gone. I had taken control, and all this newfound time had given me the chance to focus on new things and allowed me to improve, to become a better version of me, without cutting back on anything. I had gained around 15 hours of my week just by flicking off the switch to the autopilot.

I had taken back the controls and was ready to fly higher than before. There was no limit now. It didn't matter how busy I became, I knew that I was always going to have time to learn and improve. And if I didn't, it would be down to me – no excuses.

I had found a gap, an error in my way of life, and by just changing a small thing I gained so much. And you can do the same!

*'TIME CAN NEVER BE AN EXCUSE.*
*IT'S JUST A MATTER OF PRIORITY.'*

*Salvatore Bruno*

Simply by helping them to turn off that autopilot, I have shown people who believed they had no time to learn something new, to gain more time to focus on increasing their knowledge on a subject that interests them. The trick is to look closely at your life routine and see where and when your autopilot kicks in, then turn it off.

Do you commute for long periods of time?

Do you find that you have to do a lot of waiting around?

Do you travel a lot?

Do you spend a lot of time doing something where you know that you are in autopilot?

Well, let's flick that switch! It's time for you to gather up those autopilot hours and make good use of them. Once you work out the time spent in autopilot per day, you make a very easy calculation so you know how long you have gained each week to put towards whatever you have chosen to do with this time.

1. When are you in autopilot? Eg, commuting.........
2. How many minutes are you (Answer from question 1 here) for each day? .........
3. How many days per week do you do this? ......................

**Autopilot Calculation:**

*(Minutes/Hours per day) x (Days per week) = Amount of hours gained per week.*

So, now you know the number of hours per week that you have gained to learn, listen, or do whatever you wish with, go ahead and enjoy them. Make sure you focus on gaining with this extra time.

There is no point going back once you have flicked the autopilot off. You need to make sure you are always moving forward and always improving.

This simple exercise is something we can all do with our lives, but no-one can force you. I have shown you the way, as I have shown others, yet some people still just continue living life in autopilot, wasting precious time.

Always remember that life is what you make it. People like me can only show you different ways of looking at a situation, but at the end of the day, it will always be about how badly you want that dream life.

Are you willing to flick that autopilot off, take control of these times, take charge of your destiny? You are in charge of your destination, and it can be full of positivity, knowledge, happiness, and whatever you want to have.

# THE CHOICE IS YOURS!

## *Question:*

*Are you ready to take control and turn off the autopilot switch?*

# Chapter 15

# THE NUDGE!

Here comes the NUDGE! This is going to sound very strange, but it works amazingly well with the stresses of our daily lives and putting things into action.

What the hell is a nudge, you ask? If you search for 'What is a nudge?' in Google, you will find this:

'A **nudge** helps people make better choices for themselves without restricting their freedom of choice. It accomplishes this by making it easier for people to make a certain decision. In other words, putting fruit at eye-level counts as a **nudge**. Banning junk food does not.'

So how do I use a nudge, and why? A few years back, I was one of these people that struggled to make a decision or to put a new routine in place, and I found myself getting stressed about the simplest things. It was easier for me to reply 'I don't mind' when someone asked me what I wanted to eat or where I wanted to go.

I found myself falling back to the old routine as I kept forgetting about the new things I had to do, because the moment I got something on my mind it would just go into overdrive and everything was forgotten. I started wondering how I could help myself to improve my decision-making and dealing with life's daily stresses.

It would need to be something easy to remember and something I could visualise.

So, one day I overheard two people talking about their day, and one said he spent hours writing out

Post-It note messages for himself so that he knew what to tackle when he got back into the office in the afternoon.

It started me thinking. *Was it as easy as a note on a yellow sticker? Surely our minds are not that simple, or are they?*

As you know, the mind is powerful, so it doesn't need a lot to kick-start a new habit, or to take in small amounts of information while we are doing something else. Like me sitting on a plane, listening to an audiobook, surrounded by people. My mind is learning while taking in what else is going on around me.

So that's how it began. I started putting a new system in place to stick to routines, habits, etc, and a simple way to overcome the daily stresses of life. I wrote things on my yellow stickers and stuck them up around my house, on my desk, even on the dashboard of my car. I had become sticker mad! I even imagined one day waking up and my whole house covered in millions of these bright yellow sticky notes.

Then I started to think about how I could use these notes in such a way that I wouldn't need a million of them around the house, the office, or even in my car.

I knew it had to be simple but needed to have a meaning. Something I could write on this note that would remind me of something I needed to do, remind me of a time or place I needed to be, or to take a break – anything that I needed to get through my day. And I came up with a plan of action, a way to help me and my future clients to achieve a better mindset but also to have some sort of system they could use if and when they needed it.

My Post-It note system had two forms:

1. The routines, habits, goals.

2. Dealing with other things like daily stresses.

And so the nudge came into play!

With the first form, I knew I wanted to have daily reminders of my goals, reasons for getting up, and what I wanted to achieve – not because I had forgotten, but a reminder to help motivate me, a message to drive me every morning to smash the day ahead.

I wrote my list of goals/dreams on a Post-It note and stuck it onto the mirror I looked into every morning, so when I woke up and turned on the lights, I saw this list.

I have had clients put these lists on the back of their front door so that it's the last thing they see before they leave the house; or inside the wardrobe door where their coats are kept; inside a wallet, so every time they open it they see the list; on the dash of the car; or on the screen of their computer.

I am sure you are already thinking of where you could put your list. Only one or two sticky notes are needed for this – no more – as these lists work as trigger points to spark up your internal furnace.

For me, this was just the beginning. Now I have a way to kick-start my day, to motivate myself, to give me that reason to smash the gym session, to be confident in that meeting. Whatever the goal or dream is, these little reminders are in your face, making sure you don't forget why you started.

They remind you why you are walking down this path of life, and why you have made the choices that have got you to where you are now. Over the years, this has improved from being only a list of goals to including a motivational quote that fires up that inner furnace. It might be a certain line from a film that triggers your inner power. But whatever it may be, it has helped me and my clients to overcome negativity, establish new routines and habits, and helped us achieve our goals.

You might be wondering where the nudge comes in. Well, this is where the second part of this system comes into play. In part one, you had all the positive reminders which keep that fire alive, but we needed more. We were still missing something, those things that would make us take a step back throughout the day.

Our lists, motivational quotes and words, or whatever you have written down, were enough to get you started. But they are not enough to keep you on your positive path throughout the day. One negative call or situation could cause you to forget how you started our day, and that is when Part Two, the NUDGE, comes in.

The nudge plays a crucial part in your day. It allows you to give yourself a nudge to take time out, to take that step back and refocus. Imagine you are having a stressful day. There seems to be no end to it, one phone call after another, one email after another, or life is just not playing ball as it should.

Whatever the reason, you are becoming unhappy, negative, or you are beginning to struggle with the daily stresses of your day. To be honest, we have all been there and it's very easy to get sucked in, to forget to stop and take time out to refocus.

With all those pressures on your shoulders to get everything done, you feel the weight getting heavier the more time passes. You feel as if you are no longer in control and are just going along for the ride, hoping it will ease off at some point. Sometimes, though, it doesn't. One day rolls into two days, then a week, and before you know it weeks have gone by and you have turned into this out-of-control person with a huge weight on your shoulders. And the reason it's so heavy is that you have let all the little negative things in your daily life build up to become a huge mountain.

We need to remember to remind ourselves to stop, to take five minutes out to regather our thoughts, and to bring everything back into order before it all becomes too much. We must remember to give ourselves time out to regain control of our day, and of our lives.

*'ALMOST EVERYTHING WILL WORK AGAIN IF YOU UNPLUG FOR A FEW MINUTES. YOUR MIND WILL THANK YOU FOR IT.'*

*Salvatore Bruno*

Let's go back a few steps to examine the moment where it started to go wrong, where the pressure started to build... and it's right there that we STOP, and we NUDGE ourselves.

A simple NUDGE can stop the wheels from turning just enough for you to regather our thoughts and to refocus. And it simply gives you enough time to steer yourself back down the correct path. You see, a nudge won't make things go away, but what it does is allow you to take a 5-minute window to refocus, to calm those nerves, to take time out and take control again.

## A 'NUDGE' = 5 MINUTES' TIME-OUT

Use it on yourself and use it on others. I have found that it works perfectly with my clients who struggle with certain stresses in life, things that build up and become too much.

So, how can you use it? You can use it as a single word if you feel it will be enough. But for me,

I have found that the best way to get the impact of a nudge is to write it down on a Post-It note and always have it close to hand. The moment you start to feel things are getting too much, take the note out and place it in front of you – on your desk, on your computer screen, even on the phone – wherever you can see it, and it will stay there until you take your time out.

For example, you are having a stressful conversation on the phone and you know it's getting to you. Bring out the NUDGE, and when the call is over you can see you require a timeout.

Now here comes the second most important part of the nudge: take the five minutes away from where you are. If you are at your desk, go for a walk to the kitchen, or the toilets. If you are at home, same again, take yourself away from the place where the nudge is, and do not come back until you have done your five minutes' time-out.

This will allow you to gather your thoughts, regain control of your emotions, relax your heart rate, and slowly come back to your positive state of mind. You should always be able to do this within five minutes because you have that drive, that determination to be better, and you know this isn't you. With these nudges, you know how to control that negativity, and how to stand tall when things get tough.

Some people look at this as being weak and walking away from the stresses of daily life. I look at it as overcoming the stresses of daily lives; I see it as us becoming better, learning how to control the stresses, the emotions, to find the keys to unlock the true potential of our inner strength, and give ourselves the ability to overcome any situation. In my eyes, this is always going to be a winning formula.

*'WHEN WE TAKE THESE TIME-OUTS,*
*WE MAY FIND THAT SOLUTIONS*
*PRESENT THEMSELVES.'*

*Salvatore Bruno*

You have now been passed the power of the NUDGE, and this is another tool you can share with others. Use it to help family, friends, anyone you feel could benefit, or don't tell a soul and keep the power of the nudge to yourself.

The choice is yours, but use it well and learn to overcome any stressful situation that is thrown at you. Learn to overcome the negatives of your daily life and make it a more positive and happier one.

*'THE NUDGE. SOMETIMES AS ADULTS,*
*WE JUST NEED A TIME-OUT TO*
*REFOCUS AND GATHER OURSELVES*
*BEFORE STARTING AGAIN!'*

*Salvatore Bruno*

*Question:*

*Are you going to keep the power of the NUDGE*

*to yourself, or spread the knowledge?*

# Chapter 16

# THINKING OUTSIDE THE BOX!

One of my golden rules is right here: Thinking outside the box. It is one of the things I live by, and I truly believe you can have all the correct tools to stay on the right path of life and even have a great positive mindset, but you will only get so far without this part.

Picture the path life as a road: if your life is good and positive, the road will look straight, it will have beautiful views, the colours around will blow your mind, the noises make you want to sing; if your life is not good and you are negative, your road will be heading up a very steep hill which is hard to climb even at a slow pace, there are no views – just really dark, high walls on each side – there are no magical sounds, and the road just keeps going on and on in the same way.

Even if you are on an amazing path of life and are happy and positive, you might be still want to change and become the best version of yourself. To find that life you have dreamed of, you will need to dig even deeper and look beyond the views, see past the straight road, and think outside the box.

This is a skill we need to learn – it's not built into us, and you must really want it if you aim to achieve those things other people thought were not possible.

So, how do you learn it? How do you use it? And, most of all, how do you get to be one of the very few people in this world that does this?

Firstly, you must be okay about wanting more. That may sound easy enough and maybe even a little stupid, but it's not. That's because a high percentage of people get to a certain place in their life and are just happy to stay there. They believe they have found their happy place – or happy enough place – and are content to stay there. And there is nothing wrong with that at all.

But if you truly want to achieve the incredible things in life, you must always want more. You have to be willing to put the work in and to continue to look for ways to improve, to grow, and this is what will allow you to think outside the box. It's what I call the 'real animal instinct' in us, hunting to be better, to be stronger, and to be happier. Hunting to make those dreams a reality.

*'A LION IS KING OF THE JUNGLE
BECAUSE IT DOESN'T WAIT FOR
AN OPPORTUNITY. THE LION
HUNTS FOR IT.'*

*Salvatore Bruno*

If you become a hunter in life, you will always be looking at ways to improve, to better yourself, viewing things differently than others, searching for the higher road, seeking ways around the obstacles on life's road. You may even be looking beyond the road itself, and seeing all the ways to achieve anything you want.

The magic of really thinking outside the box is not what you see but what you can gain. The simple fact that you can think outside the box in the first place must never be taken lightly.

It is a gift; a power which so many people cannot and will never be able to do. There are two main reasons for this: not wanting to; and not able to. And this is where your desire to become better and truly wanting to achieve your dreams is the key.

If you always have the desire, you will always be able to think outside the box, you will always be able to hunt. Let's be honest, what good is a hunter really if he doesn't want to hunt? A wild animal hunts because it wants to feed, while we hunt for our foods of life and all the goodness it brings.

So, you now know that you must want this, but how do you use it?

Well, this is how the magic happens. It's not a flick of a switch or anything like that. You just need to make yourself hungry for that WANT! You must want to hunt, because once you are at this level you will suddenly start to see things differently, you will no longer see what others around you are seeing.

You will see other ways to achieve things and you will find it easier to resolve things, because you will not be looking at the problem but hunting for the solutions. You will no longer be telling yourself, 'I would like that.' You will be telling yourself, 'I want that!'

*'A DREAM YOU WOULD LIKE,*
*TO A DREAM YOU WANT,*
*IS A COMPLETELY DIFFERENT*
*OUTLOOK.'*
*Salvatore Bruno*

Thinking outside the box is that person who walks past everyone who is standing in the same queue as him but sees the other door open because he was searching for the open door not focusing on the closed one.

Thinking outside the box is that person who sits in a meeting and will be the first to solve a problem, because everyone is spending time focusing on the problem while he has focused on the solution and has already found it.

Thinking outside the box is the person who will never be out of work or opportunities as he is always hunting for them rather than focusing on not having work.

Thinking outside the box is the person who still achieved things and found the positives while in lockdown, when others just sat around and focused on the negatives.

Thinking outside the box is simply the person who WANTS to become the best version of themselves, and who WANTS to make those dreams a reality.

That person is you! You can be a hunter, but you need to believe, and you must truly WANT it. Don't be left behind while people around you are walking down their amazing road of life, making every opportunity that falls in front of them count. Don't be left behind as people around you talk about how they have just achieved something you want. It's all yours for the taking and you can truly have it all.

Become the HUNTER and let your inner strength help you achieve all the wonderful things you dream of, all the things you want to do, all the things you want to learn. Or let it help you become the person you truly WANT to be. Thinking outside the box is for the hunters in life. My question to you is: Do you truly WANT it badly enough?

If you are with me, then embrace it and become one of the hunters of life. Use the skill of thinking outside the box to give you everything you want.

Some things will be easier to get or achieve, but the more you open your eyes and hunt, the better your life will become. The more things you achieve, the more you get; that is the true magic right there. Because once you become a hunter and start to achieve things, you won't want to ever stop.

Life's path will just become better and better, brighter by each step, by each day, and without even realising it you will be walking down a path you wanted. You won't have been given it, though. You will have earned it, hunted for it, saw it, and went for it.

YOU made it possible!

*'YOU WILL NEVER BE WRONG FOR WANTING TO LIVE YOUR BEST LIFE.'*
*Salvatore Bruno*

To become a hunter, think outside the box and truly watch as life unfolds in front of your very eyes. Your life will never be the same again. And even better, when you look back to see how far you have come and what you have achieved since you started believing in yourself and let your positive mindset and inner strength guide you, you will be shocked. But that is the moment you should stand tall, be proud, and always remember... YOU DESERVE IT!

**Question:**

*What does your road of life look like now, and what do you want it to look like?*

# Chapter 17

# TRIP DOWN MEMORY LANE!

Some people will tell you to never look into the past, that you must always focus on the path in front of you and not to look back. But I believe those people are WRONG! That's right, I am standing up for what I believe in. And so should you.

Why do I believe this? In one way, I can see where people are coming from and why they would encourage people to stay focused on the future and away from the negativities of the past. But this is where I believe we should look at things differently.

Yes, we should look forward. I agree with that. But we must look back from time to time. You see, there is something that we must never forget about ourselves, and that's where we came from, good or bad. We should never forget why we started our journey, what made us take that first step, when we first used our inner furnace, and when we started to take control of our lives.

Let's face it, if we put all this hard work into bettering ourselves but never looked back at the achievements we made, what would be the point?

*'LOOKING BACK AT YOUR*
*ACHIEVEMENTS IS AN INSIGHT INTO*
*HOW STRONG YOU HAVE BECOME.'*
*Salvatore Bruno*

I accept that looking back can be hard. It can bring back some dark memories, one that hurt or make you sad. But then you should focus on the journey to where you are today, how far you have come, the memories along the way and, more importantly, the person you have become.

To me, looking back to me isn't something *some* people should do; I believe we should *all* do it from time to time, and I call it a 'TRIP DOWN MEMORY LANE'.

My own past has dark moments in it, times that when I look back make me feel sad, angry, and all different negative emotions. But then I see how I climbed out of those dark moments, and day by day grew into the person I am today.

So, when I look back, I don't just see dark moments. I see the things I have overcome, the huge positive moments of my life that I will never forget.

And both the negative and positive things that have happened to me are the reason I am standing right here in this spot along my path of life.

We will never really understand why some things happen to us, but the moment you understand that everything happens for a reason will be the moment you take another step closer to becoming a superhuman.

Open your eyes, let those eyes look back into the past, dig deep and unlock any emotions you may have, let them flow, and take a walk down memory lane, as far as you want. In my case, I seem to pick out certain moments depending on where I am, or on certain days of the year, like birthdays, etc.

Only this morning I went back down memory lane to think about my father. What started as a negative, because he is no longer with us, soon became a trip of amazing thoughts, with images flashing in my mind, songs, places, loads of different things. It was like my mind was replaying a film of all the amazing moments I spent with my father and the impact he had on my life, to the very last seconds of him being with us.

I could give you hundreds of different ways that I enjoy walking down memory lane. I could tell you all my stories of what I have achieved to date, and what I have lined up for the future. But this book isn't about you living my life; this book is about helping you becoming a better version of yourself.

So what we want is for you to enjoy your trips down memory lane, to look back and see how far you have come, to see that moment where you stopped and realised you wanted more, you wanted better, and all the amazing things you have done along the way.

Some of you may not have started your journey yet or even taken that first step, but don't worry. I haven't forgotten about you. The journey down memory lane is a gift – from me to you. And once you know how to truly use and control it, you will become so much better, your future will look so much brighter, the place you are standing right now will feel different, and you will feel alive and more determined to achieve more going forward.

*'SOMETIMES A LITTLE TRIP DOWN MEMORY LANE IS ALL IT TAKES FOR YOU TO APPRECIATE WHERE YOU ARE TODAY.'*

*Salvatore Bruno*

It is for this reason that 'looking back' is a must... but you must be able to control it and remember why you are doing it. There is no point doing it if you come back feeling worse, and that is why you must use it properly.

It doesn't matter how bad your life is right now, there will be moments in your past where you laughed a bit, you smiled, a point in your life where you had some positive things happening.

Now I am aware that some people don't live a life full of sunshine and rainbows, but we have all had good moments, those times in our life where things seemed a little bit better, the sun seemed a little bit brighter, and the weight on our shoulders seemed a bit lighter.

Our memories are what make us. Your whole life could be one big negative story, with not one positive thing ever happening to you. And if that is the case, I would say only one thing to you, 'Well done.' For the simple reason that you are still here and still standing to tell the tale, which means you are so much stronger than you think. It also means you are so ready to make the first step to a bright future, because you have been through it all, there is nothing you can't overcome, your inner furnace is lit, and you are ready to battle.

We are all in different places in our lives. Some of us could be walking down the same path but years apart; others may cross paths; some may be walking side by side. Whatever our situation, we are all able to overcome these day-to-day battles and to achieve what we want.

So, let's take a trip down memory lane together right now, and just see how far you have come already.

I think you will be truly surprised, as it's amazing when you look for something just how you will find it. We are looking back to learn and gain motivation, to make us stronger, and to remind ourselves what we have done so far and where we have come from.

Obviously, we are not all sitting in the same room (it would be amazing if I could see you all reading this and where you are), but we can still take a trip together.

So, I want you to stop what you are doing and let the first thing from your past pop into your head. You will be surprised how quickly it will come. Now, what is this memory?

Some are very clear, others not so much, but it is important to understand why has this memory has come up. Is it a good one or a bad one? Did it make you smile or sad?

Now, build off it. If it is a negative thought, start walking away from it. We don't want to stay around that for very long, so start to walk back. What is the next thing you remember? Did it make you smile?

Always remember that this is a positive trip, so let your mind find those positive markers in your life.

Now start to walk closer to present day. Do you have another moment pop into your mind? This time has your smile got bigger? Move away another step again, and continue this until you are back to present day.

Some trips down memory lane could take longer than others, depending on the memories. But as you were thinking back, did your mind start to highlight the positive moments?

Did things that you forgot had happened suddenly flash up?

Did you see yourself achieving things, awards, and prizes?

Did you see amazing birthday presents, or just random moments of your past that made you smile?

You need to focus now on where you are, think about how far you have already come, and use this to fuel your determination tanks. Fill them right up, as we want to walk away from the past and head into the future with more determination than ever. You are your own motivation and you can provide all the determination you need to overcome anything. You have the fire, you have the strength, and now you have the fuel.

Use those negative thoughts you might have brought back to improve yourself, to become stronger; use the positive memories you brought back to fire up that furnace; and use the past to show you how far you have come, to give you that drive to push forward, to want more, to become a better version of you, and to be determined that your future will be better than your past.

*'AFTER EVERYTHING I HAVE BEEN*
*THROUGH, I AM STILL SMILING,*
*NOT BECAUSE I AM STRONG*
*BUT BECAUSE I KNOW*
*WHAT I HAVE ALREADY OVERCOME.'*
*Salvatore Bruno*

This is your life. You can't change the past, but you can use it to change your future. You can use your past to improve who you are. Use the life lessons you have already achieved to achieve better things in the future, so that when you look back again your past becomes brighter and brighter and full of amazing memories, the present is epic, and the future is looking incredible. Do not let the negatives of your past hold you back. Use them, and make that negativity work for you.

Think of it like this. You are driving a powerful muscle car of life and it feels great. You have never been in so much control of life before, you know the direction you want to go, and it has plenty of power under the hood. Now it just needs the fuel for you to drive down your path of life... and this is the important bit.

Always remember this: a car will still run even if the fuel is not quite right. So, throw in the negative fuel, throw in the positive fuel, use it all, and now there truly is nothing stopping you; you have all you need.

**Inner Furnace = Fire/Motivation**

**Inner Strength = Power/Determination**

**Fuel = Memories of life (Positive or Negative)**

Remember the key factors and where to find them, enjoy those trips down memory lane, and there is no reason why you can't join the superhumans in this world. It's time you became UNSTOPPABLE along the path of life.

### Question:

*Where did your first trip down memory lane take you?*

# Chapter 18

## EVERYTHING HAPPENS
## FOR A REASON!

No beating around the bush in this chapter, this is something I was told by an old friend – someone who impacted my life in a HUGE way. I still remember the day it happened like it was yesterday. He was there when I was at my lowest; someone I didn't expect to hold out a hand and pick me up. We weren't even good friends before that moment, but all of a sudden, things went bad and there he was.

As I was walking up towards his house – a beautiful villa out in the countryside in the heart of the Andalucía hills – he was sitting outside his front door with his massive dog by his side. He didn't say anything to me; the look was enough.

I said, 'Thank you so much for this.'

And he just replied, 'No need for thanks. Cold beer and pizza waiting inside. I am going to be right here if you want to join me. If not, your bedroom is the one on the right. Help yourself, this is your home now.'

Just like that, I had become a house guest. I walked in and there were my beer and pizza. Even though I was hurting and things were not looking good, this kindness from a man I hardly knew was overpowering, and it took me a little while to come to terms with where I was standing and what was going on.

I couldn't just grab my things and go into the bedroom, even though I was in no mood to talk. What I wanted to do was to go outside and sit with this man who had opened his home for me – a man who held out a hand to someone who needed help. Me.

As I've said before, things in life happen for a reason, good or bad. But here I was being given what I would call a lifeline, an act of kindness that would open my eyes and outlook on life forever. This man didn't do it for money; he didn't do it to be called a hero; he didn't even do it so that we became friends. He did it because he saw a man who was down, who needed a helping hand to get up, and he did it in the only way he knew how.

Acts of kindness happen in the strangest ways and when you least expect them. When it happens, it feels like there is a light at the end of the tunnel. And this is why I always say acts of kindness are ways of passing on strength and happiness, and can be the most powerful thing you could ever do for someone.

The simple fact I remember this man and will never forget him is not because of what he did, but how he did it.

*'A TRUE ACT OF KINDNESS HAPPENS WHEN YOU ARE EXPECTING NOTHING IN RETURN.'*

*Salvatore Bruno*

What this man didn't know was what would happen as a result of his actions. But not only did he see the man he helped at the lowest time of his life grow into a stronger better human being, but he also gained happiness, a friend, and memories which no-one can take away from us. Memories like the first day my kids ran up to him and hugged him like he was part of the family, simply because he had become part of it; the first day he was introduced to my family when they came to visit.

What I didn't know at the time was that this man was alone. He had no-one, and opening his house to me that day would throw him onto a new path, one full of happiness and memories. And most of all, he knew I was forever grateful; from that moment, he would be a legend, someone I would call a true friend.

I will never forget the day when he sat me down and told me I needed to remember one thing. 'Everything happens for a reason,' he said. 'There is a reason why you are here, but you need to stop looking back now and look for the reason why and go enjoy life.'

He was so right! He had no idea at that moment how much he opened my eyes. I had been looking in the wrong direction, focusing on the wrong things, concentrating on the things I had lost, on everything negative. But right then, at that moment, he made me realise that I was never going to get any better if I didn't understand the simple fact that things happen for a reason, good or bad, if I controlled them or not. I needed to step forward... and that's what I did.

> *'EVERYTHING HAPPENS FOR A*
> *REASON. THAT REASON CAUSES*
> *CHANGE. SOMETIMES IT HURTS.*
> *SOMETIMES IT'S HARD.*
> *BUT IN THE END,*
> *IT'S ALWAYS FOR THE BEST.'*
> *Ritu Ghatourey*

Things like this do happen for a reason. We all go through situations in life that may not be nice and might even hurt us, but they make you see things in a different light, see people for what they are, or see life differently. I am sure if you look back at your own life, you will be able to come up with a few examples of when things have happened for a reason – like the moment the purchase of that house you were buying fell through, only for your dream house to come on the market; or when your friend didn't turn up that night so you were left standing alone at the bar, only to meet your future partner... There are so many examples I could quote.

But just take a couple of minutes to think: when did life throw a curveball at you, and out of a negative came a positive?

There is another way I look at things happening for a reason. I used to be the person that would sit and feel sorry for myself when something happened to me. I would be low, focusing on the negative, seeing the darkness. But now things are a lot different.

Why? Because I now know that EVERYTHING, not 'some things', happens for a reason.

If a door CLOSES, another is OPENING;

When it RAINS, it's because the SUNSHINE is coming;

We need SADNESS to make us appreciate HAPPINESS;

We need NEGATIVE so we can enjoy the POSITIVE;

Where there is BAD comes GOOD;

Where there is HATE comes FRIENDSHIP.

You see? EVERYTHING happens for a reason, and the sooner you believe this the sooner you will see why things happen, how you are going to gain from it, how to improve and learn from it, why we sit here reading this book, why we walk down the same path to work every day, when your gut is telling you that it's one of those moments where you know this is happening for a reason.

When you miss your flight and find yourself sitting next to someone who will end up being your best friend, you can sit there and allow yourself to believe this is not the case. Or you can believe that things do happen for a reason and continue to walk down your path of life, looking out for those crossroads that are there for a reason.

My life has changed paths many times, and so will yours. Not all of my changes were by choice, but they were definitely for a reason. I know if I am walking down a negative path it's because something is about to happen and something good is going to come. So, I walk down that negative path with my head held high, with my shoulders back, and with the mindset that change is coming. Because if you truly believe that everything happens for a reason, it will. That means it's only a matter of time until you meet the right person, your ideal job will come up, or you will be happy walking down a positive path of life.

*'THERE WILL ALWAYS BE A REASON WHY YOU MEET PEOPLE, EITHER YOU NEED TO CHANGE YOUR LIFE OR YOU'RE THE ONE TO CHANGE THEIRS.'*

*Angel Flonis Harefa*

'Everything happens for a reason' is not something you can do; it's a belief. It's something you must truly believe will happen when the time is right, and the power of your mind and the rest of your inner strengths will work out the rest. We are never meant to walk along life's paths without any ups and downs, but it's down to each of us how we want to deal with each situation. So the choice is yours: Believe or don't... things will happen.

I believe we must all think that we can be happy, that we can be positive, and truly know that we can come out the other side stronger and better than before. We must know that we can learn from it, we can grow, and we can continue aiming towards the life we are truly wanting. We are the ones that control the muscle car of life, and even if we get a puncture or someone crashes into us, we can fix it, we can mend, and we can remember the reasons why.

This is your life and you should be able to live it your way. And even though things will happen for a reason, you must understand that this is not a bad thing. I have taken it on as being just a part of life: it will happen, it will come, and, guess what? It will go!

To become the person you're meant to be, living the amazing life you're meant to live, sometimes you have to go through hard times and sometimes you have to be broken down so that you can learn, grow, and come back better and stronger than ever.

When times are tough, remind yourself that what is happening to you is happening for a reason, embrace it, and become the person you are meant to be.

***Question:***

*Do you remember the last time something happened for a reason in your life?*

# Chapter 19

## LIVE LIFE YOUR WAY!

One of the biggest beliefs you will have to overcome and truly understand is when I say to you, '**Live life your way.**' What does it make you think of?

I started doing this a few years back and found it to be one of the biggest and hardest steps for me personally. That's simply because there are no real guidelines, no instructions how to do it, because it's *your* life and everyone's life is different. We all have a choice whether we live life our way or just go with the flow, as most people do.

What are the rules of living life your way? None. And that's the great thing. You should be able to do whatever you want, when you want, and enjoy every moment. The idea of living it your way means there are no limits to what you do and how. For example, when you choose your holiday, do you do it because it's where you want to go or do you book somewhere that someone told you was good? Did you buy your car because your friend said it was a good car? Did you go and work for that company because you heard it was a good place to work?

By doing things this way, you are not living life *your* way; you are just taking other people's thoughts and ideas and using them in your life. Are those holidays as good as that person told you? Does that car drive as well as your friend said? Or is that company not for you after all?

Living life your way means taking that leap of faith sometimes. It can mean spending money on a car you have no idea about, or not working for anyone at all and starting your own business so you can do it your way and by your rules. Why do some couples decide that they don't want kids, and then there are others that want two or three? Why do some people prefer to be single than be in a relationship? Or why does that person walking down the street have red hair and tattoos from head to toe?

None of these people is wrong. They may choose to do things differently, but in their eyes, life is how they want it and they are living life their way.

It's like the person who scrolls through Instagram wishing he/she could be like that person in the picture/video or to have what that person has. But they are wishing rather than doing. So many people are happy to wish for things but not to work for them. Athletes, models, business icons all work towards living life their way.

The best in the business – whatever the business – will not be there because they do things by half, and they won't be wishing. They will be doing things to ensure they achieve what they want.

And this is why I am very quick to tell people that if they are not happy with something in their life, they should change it. You should not only be doing things your way, but you should also be enjoying life.

It goes back to us talking about our path of life and changing it when we want. You can make huge changes to your life or you can take small steps towards what you want. Either way, you are still living it your way and you are in control of the direction in which you are heading. And that is the most important factor about it all.

It's not about getting to the end of the path, it's about living. It's about enjoying moments and making amazing memories along the way. It's about looking back and seeing what you have achieved. It's about being able to tell people that you are living your life in the best way possible.

*'DON'T TELL PEOPLE ABOUT YOUR LIFE. SHOW THEM, AND LET YOUR LIFE BE THE STORY THEY WANT TO ACHIEVE.'*

*Salvatore Bruno*

Imagine that. Imagine the idea that life could be that bright, full of happiness, positivity, full of things you enjoy doing and achieving. Picture that life. Now write it down!

You see, if you can picture it, if you can imagine it but you are not doing it, then the WANT is there. It means you see a better life for yourself, one where you are walking down a different path.

So what needs to change? What are the things that you saw that you wish you had? What did you see that made that image so good it made you smile? What was that picture you drew in your head that filled your body with warmth?

*'THE WORLD WILL JUDGE YOU NO MATTER WHAT YOU DO, SO LIVE LIFE THE WAY YOU TRULY WANT TO.'*

*Unknown*

The other important fact we must highlight here is that if you haven't done something you wanted or haven't been somewhere you wanted, IT'S YOUR FAULT.

If you are walking down a path you are not happy with, IT'S YOUR FAULT!

If you are not seeing the things in the world you truly want to see, guess what? IT'S YOUR FAULT!

Am I being harsh? Yes. Am I opening your eyes to the fact that you may be walking down the wrong path and not going to achieve the things you deserve to? I hope so.

You see, sometimes we need to have someone stop us in our tracks and tell us the hard facts; someone to say, 'Why are you NOT living your best life? Why are you NOT living life your way?'

Life isn't made of one thing; life is made out of millions of things. Some are bigger than others, but they all add up to make our current day what it is. So what is the harm in changing a few things for the better? Will you make some wrong decisions? Yes. Will you learn? Yes. Will you become stronger and better for it? 100%.

Living your best life will take time. You can't just snap your fingers and, like magic, everything is sorted and all your dreams have come true.

I am not selling you a magic pill here. I am not telling you it is going to be easy. I am not even going to tell you that you will get everything you wish for.

I have told you that life is to be lived your way and it should be filled with positive things, but there will be some things that are just out of your reach. But that is life! It happens that way so that we keep pushing forward, we continue putting in that hard work and, most of all, it keeps us focused on the bigger picture.

So, don't settle for just living. Be proud of who you are and stand up for what you deserve. Don't just be you; be the best you can be. Light up your future and when you walk down that path, do it in a way that life knows you are coming.

When it comes to life, the harder you work, the more you dream, the more you will achieve. Be that person. Be the one who can talk about the amazing things he/she has done; be the person who can tell their own stories of what it was like changing paths for the better; be the person you owe yourself to be!

When you start your best life, it's truly amazing how your eyes will start seeing things differently, how people around you that have been trying to hold you back can no longer keep hold of you, as other people are encouraging you and pulling you towards the positive light.

Where before you would see the negative in something, now you will see the positive and know that sometimes a risk is worth taking. You will also know that failing doesn't mean you're weak; it means you have tried.

*'IT'S YOUR ROAD AND YOURS ALONE.*
*YOU MAY HAVE PEOPLE THAT WALK*
*WITH YOU, BUT NO-ONE CAN WALK*
*IT FOR YOU.'*
*Rumi*

So, dig deep into your mind and heart, find that image, find the life you truly want, and go live it. Don't let anyone or anything hold you back; don't let yourself be the reason why you haven't achieved it. Let fear run wild as you leap onto a new path heading towards that brighter more positive life, the life you want, the life you deserve, but most of all the life you CAN have.

It's there for the taking, it's there to be lived, and all you need to do is want it enough to make that first step, not worry about the doubts, the fears, or the people who look at you and ask what you are doing.

Do it your way, make your stamp on life, show you mean business and demonstrate that it's your time to take control of the direction you are going. You no longer want to walk down a path with an uncertain destination. You know where you want to go, and what you want to do along the way.

Now you slowly start a new, more confident walk – one that tells everyone around you that you are someone who knows what they want and what they are working towards. More to the point, you walk like you know which direction you are heading, you are no longer lost in the paths of life, you are ready, your time to live life your way is here.

Go live it, enjoy the journey, and remember you will always regret the chances you didn't take!

*'THE TRUE SUCCESS OF LIFE IS TO HAVE THE ABILITY TO LIVE IT IN YOUR UNIQUE WAY.'*
*Salvatore Bruno*

**Question:**
*What is the biggest thing you want to change about your life?*

# Chapter 20

# BELIEVE, AND YOU WILL OVERCOME!

I have told you this before, but we must implant this message firmly into your mind. The simple fact is that we will always come across hurdles, obstacles, things that will try to stop us achieving our goals and prevent us from making those dreams come true. This could be down to doubt, fear, people, or just life in general. Whatever it is, we must stand strong and always tell ourselves one thing.

'I CAN DO THIS!'

These four simple words make a huge difference, because if you truly believe you can, you will achieve some of the greatest things in life. Some will seem impossible, it may seem like you will never overcome your obstacle, but when you believe in yourself you are unstoppable. No job is too hard, no mountain too high, the world is yours for the taking. But you must believe this, and you must tell yourself that you deserve it.

Overcoming fear and doubt may be the hardest obstacle you will ever come across, but when you do and you learn the importance of believing in yourself, you will see some truly magical things happen. Doors will open, you will see the sunrise differently, you will feel different, you will look at negative situations with positive eyes, you will walk with proud steps – each one making a statement that you are here and you mean business.

I'm

As I have said before in this book, the choice is always yours. It will be down to you whether you achieve those dreams or not. Blaming others is just you making excuses, and we all know excuses count for nothing on the right path of life. So this is the part of the book where I push for you to do something.

I ask you to take that step, join the thousands, millions of people who are achieving some amazing things, who are living a life their way. They are the ones who said no to doubt, no to fear, and the ones who now are proudly walking down a path they chose.

PLEASE, PLEASE take that step! You won't regret it. If anything, you will thank yourself months, years down the line when you look back and see how far you have come. It won't happen overnight, but believing in yourself takes time, takes true guts, and a hell of a lot of inner strength. Believing in yourself is a gift that can't be given. You have to work for it and it has to be earned, but once you have earned it you will appreciate the moment. And you will have unlocked all your true potential. The magic key is in your hands – you just need to use it.

Some folk think I am mad when I talk like this, but let's be honest, people don't just wake up one morning as champions. They work for it, and work damn hard. But what is the main thing about a champion, something that makes them stand above the rest? They believe in themselves; they believe they are good enough to be champions; they have the magic key and have unlocked all their potential; they walk with meaning, their head held high, fear and doubt just bouncing of them as though their skin has become impenetrable.

You might not want to be a champion, of course. Your goal might be to lose a bit of weight, or to find a better job, or just to have a better life. But whatever your goal, you MUST focus on it, you MUST want it, and you also MUST believe you can do it. No matter what it is, you CAN do it, you WILL do it, and you will truly become the unstoppable force that you dream about – the kind of person you wish you could be, the person you are becoming bit by bit.

> '*YOU CAN, YOU WILL. THESE ARE THE KIND OF WORDS THAT ONLY COME FROM A POSITIVE MINDSET.*'
> *Salvatore Bruno*

I have done some things which people think are mad (see: Chapter 22, My Impossible Challenges), others have even said are impossible. But after watching videos or hearing about it, they look at me in disbelief and ask, 'How?' And I will always answer in the same way: 'I didn't believe it was impossible. I believed it was possible.'

Such a simple thought can change your whole outlook on things and on life. Imagine if every time you came across a hurdle in life, instead of thinking of the doubts and fear of overcoming it, you instead ran at it with full force. You fired up that inner power and unleashed that internal fire, and instead of walking up to this closed door, you ran through it with no doubts, no fears, just true belief that you wanted to get to the other side. No mountain is too high now, no run is too far, and no job is too hard. You have the gift, you have unlocked that true potential and let the world of opportunities open the doors for you. Never forget: if the door won't open, we can always run through them.

*'DON'T WASTE A MINUTE NOT BEING*

*HAPPY. IF ONE WINDOW CLOSES,*

*RUN TO THE NEXT WINDOW –*

*OR BREAK DOWN A DOOR.'*

*Brooke Shields*

Now that you know about unlocking your true potential, nothing can stop you. You just need to believe in yourself. Is this something too much to ask? Are you asking too much from yourself? HELL, NO!

You deserve this. Remember that.

Never forget that life is how you make it. We are all born a certain way, we are all made differently, but you grow into the person you want to be or into the person you don't want to be – that's your choice.

I like meeting people who don't believe in themselves, because I always see straight through them. I can see their true potential long before they have even thought about it, for the simple reason that I see the good in people. I love to see their eyes light up when I tell them the way forward and their inner fire spark up when I tell them I believe in them and so should they.

These people tell me about the stories of how hard life is, how unhappy they are, and how they feel weak. But when I look at them, I don't see weakness or sadness. I see someone bravely battling life's wars... but they don't have to. They believe they are losing, and that's the problem for so many of them. If you believe you are losing or failing, you already have!

*'FAILING IS NOT A SIGN OF WEAKNESS. IT'S A SIGN OF SOMEONE TRYING. AND YOU ONLY REALLY FAIL WHEN YOU STOP TRYING.'*
*Salvatore Bruno*

I have seen people make amazing turnarounds. I have even done it myself! It isn't down to fate, it is down to believing you deserve better, it is down to believing you can. And I will continue to tell people what I see in them if this is a way that I can help people have a better outlook on life, by showing them that the way they think is wrong.

I truly believe we are all capable of achieving some amazing things. We have the inner strength, the inner drive, all the ingredients just waiting to be used. And we all have the magic key which will allow us to unlock our true potential. So, why wait any longer to live the life you want?

Start to believe, and let those powers rush to the surface. Watch as your sight changes, how things around you seem different, witness how believing in yourself puts a smile on your face because you are truly proud of who you are.

You are standing tall like a true warrior of life, someone who has been beaten before and knows what the world looks like with negative eyes. But no more.

It's time to draw the line in the sand and take that step over. You can do this. Nothing and no-one can stop you becoming the best you can be, the person you have always dreamed you wanted to be.

You cannot and will not be left behind. Come and join us as we do this our way. Believing in yourself will give you no excuses, it will give you no doubts, it will push fear to the side, and most of all it will fill your whole body from top to toe with a feeling like no other. For the very first time, you have sparked up all your inner strengths and now you are truly ready for life's battle and to overcome anything it throws at you.

Life is there for the taking. Go get it!

## *Question:*

*Do you really believe in your capabilities,*

*and do you believe you deserve better?*

# Chapter 21

# MY HERO, MY FATHER!

I truly believe that throughout our lives many people will impact us in such a way that we can't explain. They will improve you, support you, and see something in you which others do not. Their words will have more meaning and the bond between you and them will be unbreakable. These people will find a way of making you understand right from wrong, and will forever have a place in your heart. These people are real-life legends, and are never forgotten.

This is the moment where I open my heart to tell you about a man who was a true legend. His smile would light up the darkest room, his heart was always open to help and support others, and he walked this planet with meaning, to be a rock to his family, friends, and anyone else that crossed his path of life. The man that I am describing is my father, and he will forever be in my heart and be the man that I call my hero.

He was truly a great man to me and our family. He worked hard and gave us everything that we needed, his big heart spreading love and happiness wherever we went. I remember hearing people telling me, 'Your dad is so lovely, so caring.' And he made time for everyone, making sure we were always safe and well.

I can honestly say I looked up to him and was always proud to call him my father. But in March 2015, something happened that would change my life forever. It shook me to my core, broke me, and affected me and my family.

On the 2nd of March, 2015, my hero, my father, passed away of a heart attack. It was a total shock to us all. I will never forget kicking down the door of the bathroom at our family home, then falling to the floor to try and revive him. I was beating down on his chest to try to bring him back from the dark side, with my mother screaming in the background as she looked on.

I would not let him go. I kept beating down on him, hoping that he would suddenly open his eyes and come back to us, but the next thing I remember is the paramedics asking me to move so they could take over. I felt helpless. I felt weak, I felt like all the life in my body was rushing out. I was just standing there watching, but deep down I knew I had failed to bring him back. I knew I was too late and my father was no longer with us.

I remember one of the paramedics telling me before they left that my father had passed away and it did not matter what I had done, I wouldn't have been able to save him. But his words were lost in the emotions I was feeling. My rock, my hero, was no longer with us, and it hit me like a high-speed train, while my mum fell to the floor as she was given the dreadful news.

I stood there numb. I wanted to do more. I wanted this situation to be different, and the reality hit hard that this was no dream, that it was actually happening, like a scene out of a movie – the only difference was I wasn't the hero in this movie. The hero was the one who was lying on the floor. My hero had gone.

There are moments in our lives that will change us; points in your life that you will have no control over. You will feel as though everything is over, like life has kicked you so hard you see no way of coming back. For me, at that very moment, there was no light, everything was going wrong, and because it was not planned, I didn't see it coming. The shock of these situations can affect you for days, months, or even years.

While I was standing there in the doorway, holding my mum, looking at my father, I had no thoughts. I was cold, I was lost, and the shock had yet to come. But one thing I did know was that life was never going to be the same again, ever.

*'WHEN SOMEONE YOU LOVE DIES,*
*IT CHANGES YOUR LIFE FOREVER.*
*IT IS NOT SOMETHING YOU GET*
*OVER. THE LOSS NOW BECOMES*
*A PART OF WHO YOU ARE.'*
*Salvatore Bruno*

To be honest, I know that it's always hard to explain such a sad situation like this. Some people never speak about it, others keep it to themselves, and some tell the story so that people understand they are not alone. I know people die every day, but when it's a loved one, when it's *your* loved one, it's a whole different ball game. And because of the person my father was, his death was something that would alter my outlook, affect my feelings for things, and in a blink of an eye change me. And this is something I had to learn and come to terms with.

I had to stand strong. I was the oldest son and that brought huge pressure. There was no room for the person I had been before. Life had taken a huge and unexpected turn, and for me to be able to continue, I had to grow, I had to adapt, and I had to improve in ways I couldn't explain. Changing when you want to is something you are in control of; changing when you have no control, is a harder battle.

You may have been through a similar experience; perhaps you, too, have lost your hero and legend. Or maybe you're lucky enough to still have your hero with you, so have not yet faced this. Trust me, it will get easier, but you need to dig deeper than ever before and become the person you were destined to become. In moments like this, people will say there is no time for weakness, but I disagree. I believe we should allow the weakness in and let all those emotions run wild, because bottling them up will affect you further down the line. It will be like a ticking time bomb waiting to go off; you have no idea when or where it will happen, but it surely will. So, this is why we need to open our hearts, let memories and thoughts flow through our minds, and let our inner strengths take charge. Then slowly you will rebuild one emotion at a time, one sad thought at a time, and you will survive... and you will learn to live life again.

As I sit here writing this book, I have been able to talk about the moment when my dad passed. Not because it hurts me, but because it is a memory that I will never forget. It was a turning point in my life that made me into the man I am today, and that is the reason why I shared that with you all. You needed to understand that I didn't just wake up one morning and things were suddenly positive.

I mentioned before that life has its ups and downs, and this was a very big down for me. But, damn, did it shape me. Talk about my father leaving me a gift! He made sure it was me that had to open that door, made sure I was home, and he made me understand that everything happens for a reason. Events like this will only make you stronger. Your mindset will change, and little things that bothered you suddenly become non-existent, the negative things in life no longer have quite the same effect. Everything was changing, and I was changing, mentally. My father had given me a final gift – a gift of life. A gift that would open my eyes and mind to the real world forever.

Even now, while I am writing this with a few tears in my eyes, a smile appears on my face as I start to think about my father's gift to me. It's overwhelming, and a powerful moment I will never forget.

I was so lucky to have such a great father, but I was also so lucky to have been giving this amazing gift. He always believed in me, and this gift has given me the belief that I can achieve anything, that no mountain is too high, that I will overcome any physical or mental battle. I am my father's son, and I am proud to be able to call myself Carlo Bruno's son.

So, yes, my name is Salvatore Bruno, and on the 16th of September, 1976, I was brought into this world with no idea of the hardship that was to come but also the amazing memories that were going to happen. We don't know what lies in front of us on our journey of life, but whatever happens, you must learn from it, you must adapt, and most of all you must learn to overcome any emotion. I am proud of the man I am today, proud of who my father was, and proud to come from such a loving and caring family.

Moments like my father's death can break you, knock you down, and the shock will turn your mind into a whirlpool of emotions. But that will pass, and your inner strengths will unlock the true potential when you need them the most.

There will seem to be no light at the end of the tunnel, but one day you will finally see a tiny dot, a small glimmer of hope that there is light there. Remember, just because you can't see the light doesn't mean it's not there. It will come. We just need to remember that if we are down at our lowest point, there is only one way to go... and that's UP!

CHAPTER 21

*'DON'T LOSE HOPE WHEN YOU ARE*
*DOWN. JUST BECAUSE YOU CAN'T*
*SEE THE LIGHT AT THE END*
*OF THE TUNNEL DOESN'T MEAN*
*YOUR FUTURE'S NOT BRIGHT.*
*KEEP GOING. YOU WILL GET THERE,*
*I PROMISE.'*

*Salvatore Bruno*

I am who I am. I made myself this way, and now it's time for you to mould yourself into the person you want to be. Look out for those gifts during life's negative points. Take them, use them, and become that person that your hero, your legend, could see you becoming.

They have always seen it in you, and now it's time for you to step in front of the mirror and see that person yourself. It's time to unleash those emotions and let them open your heart and mind, let them pave your way to your brighter future. It's time for you to grab life with both hands and say, 'It's my turn.' Show yourself you can get back up, show yourself you have what it takes to overcome any barrier, and show those loved ones – those heroes that now walk in the shadows – that you are in control, you will grow, and you will continue to make them proud.

Join me as we stand up, as we look into the shadows and thank our heroes for the gifts they have given us. Thank them for being the light at the end of our tunnel, because they are the reason we are going to walk forward with meaning and passion. We are going to show the future that we never walk alone, we come packed with emotions, memories, and the fire to succeed. We are here to make a difference.

IT'S TIME TO SHOW THE WORLD WHAT MY FATHER SAW IN ME!

*Question:*

*What has your hero, your legend,*

*taught you for life's journey?*

# Chapter 22

# MY IMPOSSIBLE CHALLENGES!

We have to set ourselves up with impossible challenges. We need to push past our limits, proving to ourselves that nothing is impossible when we have grit and determination. With the right reasons and the correct mindset, everything is possible and you will achieve some amazing things.

After my father's passing, I decided that I wanted to do something in memory of him, but also something that would push my limits and prove to myself that I can do it.

I wanted him to look from the shadows and be proud of what I have achieved, so I decided the easiest way for me to do this was in challenges. Initially, I thought these challenges were only physical, but no-one could prepare me for what was to come and the mental battles I was going to have to face.

## My Challenge – 2017

In 2017, I and the V2 team organised a charity truck pull. I know this is something that has been done hundreds of times by the world's strongest men athletes, but for me it was new, it was different, and it was going to push my limits physically. I wanted to make an event that people could come to, and to be part of this special day.

One thing was for sure, I was no strong man. I am around 6ft 1in (186cm) and was weighing in around 78kgs. So even though I had spent three months focusing all my time on strength training and techniques, I was not built like a 'strongman'. This was going to be challenging, but something I needed to achieve.

After months of training, the day arrived. I hadn't had much sleep as I was very nervous – not because I was worried about letting people down, but because I had worked so hard up until this moment that I didn't want to fail. I didn't want to fail my hero.

As we pulled into the car park in Brentford just outside London (UK), I came face-to-face with the truck, and it quickly all became very real. But we had a game plan and we knew what had to be done. As people started to arrive, I got my game head on and knew I had to focus mentally.

No more smiles, no more chatting. I was becoming more and more focused as I paced up and down the 25-metre strip, which allowed me to visualise myself pulling this truck. I knew that at this point there was no turning back and I had to get the job done. I had to do what I came to do.

The announcement was made… and it was time. I remember walking up to the truck and turning around as my cousin Amadeo connected the rope to my harness. I looked up to the crowd and my team: we were all ready.

I took a couple of seconds to focus on the finish line at the end of the strip. That was my line, my focal point, where I needed to get to. And with that in mind, I took a huge deep breath, and dug my feet into the ground and one foot after another took me closer to the line. I felt no weight; I was numb with adrenalin and excitement.

Before I knew it, I could hear the clapping from the people around me. I had done it… but I wasn't finished. You see, the challenge wasn't just to pull the truck. It was to see how much I could pull – more than I had trained for; more than I could think possible. I wanted to do what I, my team, and my family all thought was impossible.

So, back went the truck to the starting line as the crowd was told that I would be attempting another pull, but this time, we were going to be adding a car – a weight that I had not attempted before. I remember the look from my osteopath Sam Hall; no words were needed. I knew he was the man to tell me if this was a good idea or not. He had the power to say 'no more', but he could see my determination and drive, and he knew I wanted this. So, he strapped me up, and once again I focused on looking down the strip at the finishing line.

This time, when I saw my family's faces, I could see that they believed I could do it. I could see in my partner Karolina's eyes that she knew I could do it, and that's the moment when I remembered why I was doing this, why I had a truck and car strapped to my back. A vision of my father came flooding into my mind and I could feel the adrenalin making my whole body tingle. It was a feeling I had never had before. I was ready, I looked over to Sam and my brother David, and told them, 'Let's do this!'

Without any hesitation, I started to pull... and the weight of the truck and car hit me. BANG! I felt it pull my shoulders back, but I drove every bit of power through my body until it reached my feet, powering them down into the ground. Suddenly I started to move forward. I was pulling it! I could hear my team shouting at me and I could see the markers on the ground pass underneath me one by one.

I looked up and could see the finishing line getting closer. I was doing it, and I knew right then that nothing was going to stop me. As I crossed the finishing line, I fell to my knees. My body was just drained, because I had just given it everything, but as I got up, the smiles around me were infectious and I found myself beaming with the joy of what we had just achieved.

But what happened next was something no-one had bargained on. While I was being checked over, surrounded by the team and close family, I looked at what I had just achieved and realised that this moment would never happen again. The thought ran through my head, *What would happen if we did it one more time?*

And that's exactly what I said to the team. 'Can we do one more pull?' My mother's face fell, as though she wanted to say I had done enough, but the others were with me. They knew I had more in me.

'Enough in the tank for one more, Bruno,' said my brother-in-law Chris.

Then out of my mouth came the words, 'Let's add more weight!' I wanted to do something that people would look at and think, *How on earth?* So, I told the team to add as many people as we could to the car and truck; load them up.

As I watched people from the crowd climb onto the back of the truck, I wasn't nervous. Something had happened during my last pull – the belief I could do this. And I knew that belief was the key.

As I it was in slow motion, my brother David told me everything was ready, and I walked around to see what I was going to attempt to pull. It was crazy – the truck and car were full of people!

But there wasn't an ounce of fear in my mind. I knew that one of two things could happen: I would manage to pull it, or I would try but fail. However, I knew I would rather fail than not try at all.

There I was, for the third time that day, standing in front of the truck and looking down the strip to the finishing line. This time, though, my thinking was different. I knew that my load was going to be heavy and it may not move, but my thought was just to try, to dig deep and give it everything I had just to move it. That was all.

I suddenly stopped focusing on the end, and instead focused on my feet. I started to visualise the power going through my body and forcing my feet to go through the ground. With my mind ready, I gave the thumbs up and the countdown started. People were staring at the truck, focusing on the wheels. Would they run? Would the truck move?

5, 4, 3, 2, and 1... Down I went, and I gave it everything. The weight was painful and held my body in one place. I pulled and pulled, but nothing... the truck was solid, as though it was stuck to the ground. People were screaming but I could not hear anything.

Suddenly images of my father ran through my mind, and it was like a boost of energy running through my body. I let out all my rage in a massive scream and pulled. At that very moment when I thought I wanted the truck to move, I felt myself jar forward as if my foot had slipped. But it hadn't slipped... it had moved forward, then the other foot did the same. I was moving.

From somewhere, I could hear my brother's voice shouting right in my ear, 'COME ON! COME ON!' He knew the battled had started, and so did everyone else. As I slowly inched my way up the stripe, the spectators followed, screaming encouragement.

The weight felt as though it was getting heavier with every step, but I knew I could not stop. I had to continue. I looked down at the ground and saw the halfway marker!

Looking up briefly, I saw what I was now aiming for. The finishing line was in my sights. Placing one foot in front of the other, bit by bit I dug deep and used every bit of determination, fire, and inner strength I had and slowly crossed the finish line. As I did so, I collapsed to the floor, my body zapped of every bit of energy I had. But one thing was clear...I DID IT!

I had wanted to prove to myself that limits are there to be broken through; I'd wanted to achieve something that I thought was impossible for me. But after that day, I knew that if you really believe in yourself and truly believe in your inner strengths, you can overcome some amazing things.

I remember looking around at everyone, thinking to myself that my life was going to be different from then on. This had been another big step for me on my life's path, my first challenge, and it opened the doors to what was coming next. I still admit I am no strongman, but in the battle of Man vs Machine back in March 2017, I won – and that was enough for me.

V2 Charity Truck Pull 2017

Final Pull – 6.5 tons

Distance – 25 metres

Charity – British Heart Foundation

Film - https://youtu.be/tErLNM1sVxc

So, what to do next? Where could I go from there? I decided it had to be something different, so the following year we came up with a new challenge, one we knew was going to push my mind and body even more. I was going to attempt something that hadn't been done before, and I wanted to bring something different.

I wanted to do it my way, to tell a story, to design each challenge to have its unique touch, making it different and memorable.

But I wanted people to know why I was doing these challenges, and how I would find the mental strength to overcome them. That's why my 2018 challenge was very different. It would take me to hell and back mentally, but it would also take me and the team on a journey we will remember forever.

## My Challenge – 2018

This challenge was going to be very different, including everything from the logistics to the food I would need to eat. The training was an intense four months, working closely with my coaches. We had an idea of what was to come, but deep down we had no clue how this challenge would affect us all.

I have always said that I am very lucky to have a great team to support me, but this time they had to do something they had never done before – to look after a guy on a bike as he rode down most of the United Kingdom.

My challenge in 2018 was an endurance cycle ride… with a twist. We wanted to adapt it so be something NO-ONE had ever done before, but at the same time to make a statement and create a memory that would stay with us forever.

So, in April of 2018, we planned for me to ride from Edinburgh Castle in Scotland to Windsor Castle, England. If our plan was correct, it would be around 430 miles (692km). Although that is a distance that many cyclists have done before, I knew I could make it unique in our very own way, and that's what we did.

For a start, we did it on a hybrid mountain bike. We knew that all the cyclists who had carried out these endurance rides before would have used super-light road bikes, so using a bike which was a lot heavier and not everyone's first choice would be a start to making this challenge different. However, the biggest statement we wanted to make was that this challenge would be non-stop!

Now, I know that is a big statement to make. I had a picture in my head of how it would go: for me, that was to cycle down the country and arrive in Windsor in a time that no-one could believe possible. *Imagine if I could do the whole journey with no sleep!*

Of course, we put rules in place for health and safety reasons, so I was able to stop for toilet breaks and things like the law of the land, traffic lights, etc. We even planned to stop briefly for food breaks, because we knew this wasn't just a race – this was going to be a battle of endurance, a battle of the body and mind, and this was going to be a battle that I needed to win.

On the 19th of April, the support team and I left Windsor to start the drive up to Scotland. We had two vehicles, and I had an epic team: Andy and Sarah Webb, Richard Axtell, my partner Karolina, and our very own film man Michael Edwards.

We drove up laughing and chatting away on the radios, but while everyone was enjoying the trip, my mental battles had already started. In my head, I was thinking, *This was wrong; this was my first mistake.* On a map, the country can look small, so when you plan checkpoints along a route it doesn't seem very far from point to point. But when you sit in a van for hours up and down hills, the impact of

MY IMPOSSIBLE CHALLENGES!

how far you have to ride really hits you. The realisation that you have to ride back means that doubt starts to enter your mind.

*I don't think I can do this.* These words were running through my head over and over again. My mind had already started playing games and it was winning... and I hadn't even started yet.

I decided to rest my eyes and not look out of the window, so I put my headphones on and zoned out. I knew I had to sort my mindset out, otherwise I was going to lose before I had even started, because we all knew this would be a huge battle of the mind as well as a physical one.

Off I went to my special place – the one I go to when I need to regroup. Thoughts of my kids, my father, family, friends, everything positive flowed through my head, and just like that I was imagining riding back through Windsor. I could picture myself finishing the challenge, riding up towards the castle with my family and friends there to support me as I stretch out my hands to touch the gates.

*Did I just visualise myself completing this challenge? Was this my mind telling me I could do this?*

I remember hearing the others say we had arrived at the borders of Scotland, and all of a sudden I didn't feel worried. The journey now felt different. I was looking out to hills, but not ones I feared; all I could see was the sun shining and views for miles around. I realised that this ride was going to show me some of the most beautiful scenery that the UK had to offer, and I was once again positive. I was ready.

Before we went to bed that night, we sat down and had a meal together, talking about the challenge ahead but mostly laughing. Right then, I knew

I could not fail this team. My training was over, we had a plan, and we all knew that at 4.30am the next morning we would be leaving Edinburgh Castle on a journey which no-one had ever done before. We were all really excited.

The morning came round quickly, and as we left the hotel and started our short drive to the castle, I felt overwhelmed, as though my father was watching me, saying to me, 'Good luck, son' with his big smile. The image filled me with joy.

The team unloaded my bike. I was ready; we were all ready... It was time!

At 4.30am on the 20th of April, 2018, I reached out my hand and touched the gates of Edinburgh Castle. Then I started to pedal my way out onto the dimly-lit streets of Edinburgh. I could feel the cold of the Scottish night, but with the support vehicles lighting up my way, it felt like I was in a dream.

I wasn't sure if I had started my ride or I was I dreaming it. *Would I suddenly just wake up and still be in my hotel room?*

The feeling is hard to explain, but imagine that you know what the journey is, where the checkpoints are, and the final destination, but you also know that there are so many battles to face and many unknowns to handle. That was how I felt.

I was excited but couldn't help being anxious about what was to come, with little pockets of doubts creeping into my mind. But I did what I do best: I pushed these to one side and focused on the now. I couldn't worry about things I didn't know about. I had a game plan and that was to focus on my checkpoints; we'd broken the country down into small steps to overcome this huge challenge, and I was going to ride it in small sections, never focusing on anything more than the actual stage I was riding.

It's safe to say, you can be the world's most positive person, have the best team behind you, and yet things will still happen which will make you doubt your capability. As we made our way out of Edinburgh and the sun began to rise, I was in trouble and I knew it. Hills after hills! Scotland wasn't showing me any nice views and it wasn't offering me any big downhills. I had been riding for hours and it felt like I had got nowhere, my legs were burning. I knew my pace was well off, and I was struggling.

All I kept thinking was, *Surely this can't be it?* The image of me stopping and ending the challenge made me shiver with fear. Mind battle two was coming, and we were still only on Friday morning.

We'd planned to leave Edinburgh Castle at 4.30am so that we could reach the Pennines before nightfall. The ultimate goal was to be in Windsor around Saturday evening so that I would only have to deal with one full night of cycling. Two nights of cycling with no sleep was not an option, but I was already falling behind. The slower my pace, the further the hours got pushed back.

I clearly remember my first real mental breakdown on this challenge. I stopped for a quick refuel break but also because my legs were on fire, yet I didn't want to tell the team I was struggling. I didn't want to come across as weak, but they could see the pain on my face.

As they told me about the stats of how I was doing, the reality hit me like a ton of bricks. I had ridden so slowly that if I continued at the same pace, we would arrive in Windsor on Sunday afternoon! I wanted to cry, but the team didn't allow that. They started making silly jokes and throwing sweets, bananas, bagels with jam down my neck; they knew how to build me back up. If it wasn't for their support at that moment, I probably would have quit there and then. The harsh truth hit me: this was a battle I could actually lose.

We'd known that mental and physical break-downs would come and we were sure we would get back up. But when you have miles and miles in front of you, and still have the highest point to get over, it hits you hard. But the message from them was spot on, as they urged me: 'GROW A PAIR, BRUNO, AND LET'S GET THIS DONE!'

I got back on the bike and, like a man on a mission, I powered my way to the next stage – to hit the Pennines before nightfall. Nothing else mattered now; that was my checkpoint. With this new game plan, I didn't feel any more burning in my legs, my mind and I were on the same page once again, and we knew we had a job to do.

As we approached the bottom of the climb that would take me up the Pennines, I didn't think twice. I kept my pace steady and up I went, bit by bit, higher and higher. The roads were unbelievable – the smoothest I have ever ridden on – and all I kept thinking was that I was doing it, I was getting there, and the sun had not gone down yet. I was back in the game.

We arrived at the top and something was telling me to stop. As we all turned to face the sun setting, we could see for miles. The view was incredible, the moment felt surreal, and everything that had happened up until that moment was suddenly forgotten.

We were still a little behind time, but as I stood there at the highest point of the mountain, watching the sunset, that no longer mattered. I knew my father was watching me, and I knew he was with me. I started to cry, as though every emotion came to me at once – sadness, happiness, fear, excitement.

We were standing at the top of this mountain, surrounded by patches of snow and watching the sun going down, I knew we were making special memories. And at that point, I knew I would not fail them. I couldn't let my team down, my family down; I couldn't let my father down.

I got back on the bike, feeling recharged, and remember telling the team, 'Let's do this!' I knew I was standing at the highest point which meant we had a lot of downhills to come. Now I needed to knuckle down and make up that time. I had a job to do, and I planned to do it... and off I went.

I was full of determination as I kept my head down and my feet moving as I cycled along these amazing roads. As the night came, I just rode faster, my pace got quicker and quicker, and I was back in my comfortable rhythm. I didn't feel anything. For the first time in the challenge, my mind was blank; it was fully focused on the job in hand.

Hour after hour, I pushed through, the temperature dropping below zero as we reached further into the night. This was the battle I had been expecting and I knew it would be the hardest part of my challenge, yet I felt like I was ready for it.

My team were shouting messages from the van, reading live Facebook feeds to keep me motivated and messages that people were sending. I heard them all and the support fuelled me to keep my pace steady. During that night, I recorded some of my best ride times, as though I knew that once that sun came up I was no longer on Friday.

I had no idea of time or where we were; I just cycled. At one point, the van came alongside me as I passed them my frozen drink bottles so I could replace them with drinks that weren't cold, and Karolina asked if I was okay. I didn't need to reply, though. She knew I was on a mission and I was gunning for that sunrise.

Then out of nowhere it happened. The darkness became lighter, the coldness was going, and I felt warmer. I could feel my face and hands again. I knew I was cycling into the morning, and even though I had no idea of the time, I knew I was riding in Saturday, not Friday, and it just gave me a huge adrenaline rush.

I requested more sweets and more fuel. I was in the zone, and even though my body had started to seize up due to the cold night, I didn't care. I could feel my aches and pains as my body started to warm up, but none of that mattered. I was hunting for that sunrise and I knew it was coming. I was determined to ride into it.

Just like that, the darkness had gone and we were all welcomed to the sun. I felt as though it had come up to say 'Hello, and well done.' At that moment, my biggest fear coming into this challenge had suddenly gone. The night was no longer and we had got through it, but there was a big question I needed the team to answer: Would there be another night?

They decided it was time to stop and have some breakfast. I have never enjoyed a cup of tea with a million sugars and endless amounts of pancakes with syrup so much in my life. While I was drinking it, the tea was warming up all the parts of my body which were still frozen. And the pancakes? Let's just say they didn't last long.

When the team told me what we had achieved during the night and the distance we had covered,

MY IMPOSSIBLE CHALLENGES!

I was overwhelmed and I truly couldn't believe we were back in the game. Andy assured me we were looking at finishing that day!

The final part of the journey passed without any issues. Of course, my body was broken, I was exhausted – we all were – but after cycling for that long, I just wanted to finish. So we set off with everyone full and me fuelled and high on energy drinks. It was time for action.

Off we went. No dramas, hour after hour passed, mile after mile. I was enjoying myself... and then suddenly I came across an area I recognised. The buzz was insane and the hairs on the back of my neck stood up. I knew I was getting close; we were nearly there. I could almost taste it. I was nearly home.

Everything I had done to this point began to feel like a dream. I was now only an hour away at home, and I couldn't stop smiling. I knew that very soon I was going to be joined by my coaches, Seb and Kat, plus our friend Laura, to ride the final five miles into Windsor.

When they rode up to join me, there were smiles all round. We had spoken about this moment many times, and now it was here. And off we went to finish off what we had started as a team.

As we climbed the final hill towards the castle in Windsor, I could hear Richard tooting the horn and Karolina shouting from the van, 'YOU CAN DO THIS!' I could see a crowd by the entrance – it was my family and friends, all cheering.

The whole moment was like a dream. I felt no pain, as huge amounts of adrenalin rushed around my body, and I rode on towards the gates of the castle then reached out my hands to touch them.

When my hands finally touched the gates, the cheers got louder and it all suddenly felt very real. It felt so overwhelming that I broke down in tears.

One man, one bike, one team!

Together, we had just made the impossible possible. And we proved that you can achieve anything, if you truly believe. As we stood by those ancient gates, celebrating with everyone, one thought went through my mind: *WE DID IT!*

> V2 'Castle to Castle' Endurance Cycle 2018
>
> Distance – 432 miles (694.80km)
>
> Ride time – 39 Hours
>
> Calories burnt – 26,100
>
> Charity – British Heart Foundation
>
> Film - https://youtu.be/jzs7YJ0aCsI

True battles don't come when you expect them. They come when you are broken, when you are down, and when you think that you have failed. And that is the moment when, if you look deep inside, you will find that hidden strength that you need to overcome any battle.

## My Challenge - 2019

After my mental and physical battles of the last challenge and knowing what I had achieved, the team and I decided to sit down and plan for a challenge in 2019. The whole idea of me doing another endurance cycle ride was something that excited me. I knew we had still so much to learn and I was confident that we could come up with a challenge that would push my mind and body in a whole new way.

And that's how the idea of a 48-hour indoor endurance challenge came to light.

It wouldn't be like my challenge in 2018 where the distance was the test – from one point on the map to another. This challenge would be all down to the clock. It would start at 48 hours and, bit by bit, we would count down until I had finished. Our minds made up, and it was time to prepare a game plan on how I was going to overcome this monster challenge.

Once again, I teamed up with my coaches Seb Thies, and Kat Morris, to come up with the ultimate training plan – one that would involve four months of five cycle sessions per week; my longest training session of the week being a 5-6 hour indoor cycle. It didn't take long for me to discover that this was a whole new ball game. It was going to be much harder than the previous challenges, and just like that my doubts started to appear.

*Had my challenge in 2018 been a one-off? Was I taking on too much?* Questions I knew that I didn't have the answers to ran through my mind, but the harder I trained the more Seb pushed me. I remember his words, 'We are going to make your training difficult so it will make your challenge easier.' I didn't know if that was going to be true, but these sessions were hard. Although some were only for an hour, I was cycling at my maximum, while others for five hours were at around 85% of my max effort, with nothing to look at but the inside of a gym or cycle studio.

This time, there were not going to be any amazing hills with views for miles, and no enjoyable downhills. This would be me cycling for 48 hours inside a gym, and the doubts hit me hard.

The trust between any coach and client is super important. Even though we are all friends and the V2 team are nuts, I trust them with my life. I know they were all aware of how big the challenge was, and I knew no-one was taking it lightly. So, with team talk after team talk, I became more confident, I became stronger on the bike, I was completing all my training, and I did not fail a single session, even when I didn't want to do it.

I decided to get up at 4.30am to get the job done. No-one wants to spend five hours on a Saturday in a hot spin studio while the weather is beautiful outside, but the fact was I needed to get used to being indoors, used to cycling when people were coming and going. Every time my session was finished, I walked out of that studio soaking as though I had just had a shower, but I felt amazing because I knew I was one step closer to the challenge.

Anyone who knows me knows I love my food. The HUGE bonus when you are doing this type of training and burning massive amounts of calories, if that you get to eat A LOT! So, the massive bonus of cycling indoors was that I could eat whenever I wanted – not like my 2018 challenge when it was hard to eat, especially if I was cycling up a steep hill.

We had a plan of how often I would need to eat during the 48-hour challenge to keep my body fuelled, so one of the bonuses of training like a mad man was that I could eat while cycling. Yes, I know it doesn't look that good when someone walks into the gym or spin studio and there is a guy cycling while eating all sorts of amazing foods. But this wasn't a game. We knew we needed to fuel my body like an old-fashioned steam train, and my food was the coal.

We needed to find the right food and the right times to eat to ensure I continued to move along nicely. Nothing that would spike my body too much, but food that would give me all the nutrition I needed for such a challenging event.

This meant that as much as I had to train to cycle, I also had to try out different foods while cycling. Sounds fun, right? It was. I loved it knowing that after burning around 3500 calories on a Saturday session, I could go home and eat again. I was truly enjoying this style of training.

My intake of food on my training days was up to around 8000 calories per day just to keep my muscle mass and size. The added bonus of the challenge was that I was learning so much more about my body. I was learning which fuel worked for me, what gave me that extra boost when I needed it, when to use that boost, and when not to.

I was also beginning to listen more to my body, feeling each muscle as my legs went round and round, learning that my right side pushes so much more than my left, how my lower back locks into place after a while making it key to change position, discovering that my shoulders would also lock up because I am not the most relaxed person in the world, so gripping onto the handlebars was not an option. I needed to just lean onto them and relax my upper body.

All the little things I was learning were making me able to improve my cycling and my strengths, but also my outlook on this challenge. My mental strength was growing just as my body was, and I was becoming better in every way.

The four months actually passed really quickly and I began to look forward to the challenge, talking to people in the gym about it, watching their faces change when I told them what I was about to attempt. I didn't get that disbelief from the team, though. They were confident and ready. We had everything we needed, so there was nothing to stop us now – or was there?

The problem when you push yourself on challenges like these is that things can go wrong. On my 2018 challenge, I had an issue with my knee. Actually, it was with my IT band (The Iliotibial band), which is a muscle that crosses the knee – sometimes known as cycling knee – and can play up when you over-train or cycle for long periods.

I'd had no problems since my recovery in 2018, but then one morning I woke up and could suddenly feel it. I knew it was coming back and that I had to get it sorted asap. Lucky for me, I have an amazing osteopath on the team called Sam Hall, and he went straight to action.

I had been far too confident up until this point, so this was my body saying that I needed to prepare for what was to come. I think it was the wake-up call I needed to give the challenge the respect it required. I knew this was going to be a hell of a mountain that I would need to climb slowly but firmly.

Now that I was ready, physically and mentally, it was game time once again!

On Friday morning, August 9th, I went into the Five Star gym in Windsor – the location for my challenge, and my home for the next few days. The owner, my good friend James Reedman, greeted me with a big smile and said, 'You ready?'

Everyone could see I was on a mission. I knew what was waiting for me, I had my plan, and mentally I had broken down the challenge into sections. But as I watched the team set up the bike and equipment, the gym started to become a very small room. It suddenly became very hot, and once again my mind wanted to throw some doubt around.

It was trying to make me worry, but I was so much stronger now than the previous year. So, this time I simply smiled, put my music on, and focused. There was nothing that was going to stop me. I didn't want to just complete this challenge, I wanted to show it who was boss. I wanted to make my mark, and I knew that there was no way I could fail my team, my family, and of course the big man in the shadows who was overlooking me every step of the way.

My go-time was noon, and we were only a few minutes away. I got onto the bike, looked at the big timer on the wall being set to 48 hours, and then the countdown started... 10, 9, 8, 7, 6, 5, 4, 3, 2... and 1.

I took a deep breath and my challenge was finally underway. Off we went into another journey, another adventure. I was about to have the biggest battle of my life and I thought I was prepared and ready.

'IN YOUR DARKEST MOMENTS IS WHERE YOUR TRUE STRENGTHS WILL SHOW THEIR BRIGHTEST LIGHT.'
Salvatore Bruno

We had planned out when I would eat, how to keep me hydrated, and even down to when the team would do their shift swaps. And we'd set up the computer to grab all the data from my turbo trainer, and of course to ready my stats.

I was calm, I was in a good place, time was just ticking away, and it was all going ok.

I should have been eating every 15 minutes, but my body didn't want to eat. I'd spent all those hours practising eating while cycling, and now my body didn't want to play ball. It wouldn't let me digest my food, and trust me, when you try to force yourself to eat while doing an activity, it makes you want to be sick. As that was something I didn't want to do, I didn't eat and carried on.

Hours went by, and I was beginning to feel weak. I could feel that my body was empty and needed fuel, but my body was refusing to take it. The game plan we had worked on for months was not working, and the team gathered round to work out a new strategy to solve the problem while I began to lose focus. I couldn't engage in the conversation and looked grey as my body became weaker and weaker. We needed to change things up; I had to refuel.

You've got to love how plans fall apart! There I was cycling away, with over 50,000 calories of food around me, yet my body was refusing it all. I was even becoming dehydrated as the thought of drinking made me want to be sick. And then it happened.

You obviously can't prepare 100% for these challenges, as something unexpected is always going to happen, but it's about being able to think on your feet and think out of the box when it does. And that's exactly what the team did.

Suddenly, I could smell something. When I looked up, Karolina was standing in front of me with a huge bowl of noodles and a lovely cup of tea. Okay, it's not the best fuel, but seeing something that looked light and warm was enough to put a smile on my face, and who can say no to a nice cup of tea?

Safe to say, the noodles didn't last long and before long I started eating my way through my 50,000 calories food supply. As a result, the colour came back to my face, I was feeling fuelled and I was engaging in conversation again. I felt like I was back in the game, and the great thing was it was coming up to 3am.

In a few hours the sun would be coming up, my first night would be over, and I was so ready to battle Saturday. I was looking forward to it because we'd arranged to have friends and family visit me. Before the challenge started, I had envisaged that the second night would be my worst, but after the night I'd just gone through I was no longer so sure.

I was in the zone again and things were looking good, until once again we hit something we hadn't planned for.

Early on Saturday morning, my Achilles tendon started to flare up, my ankle was swollen, and it became very painful every time I pushed down on my foot. I hid the pain for as long as I could, but eventually I explained what was going on to Karolina and my osteopath Sam. Straight away Sam examined it and said it wasn't good and we had to make a decision. So, I stopped cycling, got taped up, and started to ride again. A few hours went by but the pain just got worse and worse.

I knew that Karolina and Sam had the power to cancel the event, but I didn't want to stop at this stage due to injury. At one point, Sam made me get off the bike again as he could see on my face that something was wrong. He told me, 'If you can't walk to the toilet without the support from someone else, I am going to call this off.'

He and Karolina looked worried and I knew he meant it. I was in tears, desperate not to fail everyone. I told them, 'This can't end. I will not fail.' And I begged them to come up with a new plan.

After the team spoke, they came up with a solution that they believed would work, though it would slow me down. Desperate to grab at any light at the end of the tunnel, I put their plan into action straight away.

What was this amazing plan? I simply stopped pedalling on that foot. Sounds simple, eh?

I was more powerful on the right so not using that side felt strange, but I had no option. Pushing with my left side, around and around my feet went.

Rattling with the amount of painkillers, I was actually smiling. It was working. I was making progress again, even though it was slow, and once again the team had come up trumps at helping me head towards the end goal.

This isn't about the injuries or me being some sort of hero. If anything, I am the opposite. Looking back, it could have been a lot worse, and it was stupid of me not telling my team the moment I felt something was wrong. The real heroes of this tale are the team – every single person who kept me awake, fuelled and hydrated, motivated, and most of all kept me on that bike cycling. And as time went on and we headed into the Saturday night, things were looking good once again.

We even shared a pizza to highlight how far we had come, and as I looked around the gym at friends, family, and the team all talking, smiling, and laughing, I knew it didn't matter if this challenge ended right then. What was important is what we had already achieved.

We were coming up to the 30-hour mark and we were having a blast. Together we had made some memories that none of us would forget, and with that mindset, I continued cycling away. The night came, the team swapped shifts again, and I prepared myself for a long night ahead. I wasn't worried, because I knew I was in good hands and I that there was nothing wrong with failing.

I had given the challenge everything I had, and if it proved to be not good enough then there was nothing else I could have done.

I remember it was dark and I was watching a film, just focusing on getting through the night, when I suddenly felt myself falling asleep. I had got to the point where the nutrition was fuelling my system, but after being awake for nearly 40 hours everything was shutting down and my body wanted to sleep. I nearly head-butted the handlebars as I couldn't hold my head up.

Immediately, I shouted to Jaime Webb, 'It's time!'

We had a plan for this moment, and he knew what he had to do. We had run the whole challenge until then with hardly any caffeine or stimulants so that I wouldn't have spikes or comedowns, but it also meant that when I got to this moment we had all the caffeine and stimulants we needed. So, the film went away, out came out the loud music and cans of Monster, Red Bull, packets of sweets and bars of chocolate. My body was about to get a huge boost and we just hoped that we could ride it out until the clock hit zero.

It worked. I was fired up. No more sleepy Bruno. I was like a man possessed; I was the Mad Rider riding out the dark; I felt alive, focused, and determined to see that sunrise.

And eventually, we all watched as the gym lights went off and the sun came fully up. I knew then that it was Sunday – my final day. I had less than six hours to go and I could taste the victory.

I couldn't feel my feet, most of my body was numb, but I didn't care. We all knew we were going to make it, we just had to make sure we kept me high on caffeine, sweets, and whatever else I could throw down my neck. As the end drew near, more and more people came into the gym and the crowd started to form around me, watching as the clock entered the final hour.

We were all buzzing. Adrenalin was flowing through every inch of my body as the clock hit 59 minutes. No more hours; I only had minutes left, and I couldn't hold back the smiles. Surrounded by friends and family, once again we had achieved something incredible.

Together we watched that clock hit the minute mark, and I remember thinking of my father, why I'd started this journey and the strength that he has given me. When times were hard, he would hold out a hand and help me up. And during this challenge, we had battled the nights, overcome the negatives, and when my body struggled we pushed through and overcame it with inner strength and an unbreakable mindset.

Sometimes it's not about the things you achieve but how you achieve them, and the memories you make along the way with the people you love.

Then the clock started its final countdown. The people within the gym began to shout: 10, 9, 8, 7,

6, 5, 4, 3, 2... We all threw our hands in the air, as everyone shouted the final number...1! And just like that, it was over.

I was helped off my bike slowly, as my body was broken but my mindset was stronger than ever. Wearily, I embraced the team and the family and friends that had come along. Thanking every single one of them, I was floating with joy and excitement, honoured to stand on this gym floor surrounded by so much positivity and love.

I remember thinking how lucky I was to have this, and I smiled from ear to ear as I raised my hands once again in the air and shouted, 'WE DID IT.'

V2 48-Hour Indoor Endurance Bike Ride 2019

Total Time: 48:16:24

Distance: 565.5km

Charity – British Heart Foundation

Film - https://youtu.be/IgKWGLaK2VY

There are so many things I have learned from these challenges – how my body will adapt and how my mind will play games with me, but it will become the ultimate tool when I need it the most. And if you truly believe in yourself, you can achieve some amazing things. Life is there for the taking, so you can do what you wish with it. You can simply just walk along with it with a smile on your face, or you can step up and make memories with others, too.

I know the best is yet to come, and I know that we all have an unbreakable strength within us, but the only time you get to see it is during your darkest moments when you need it the most. Never doubt your abilities, and go do what others said you wouldn't, show yourself and others what you can achieve, and make life whatever you dream it should be.

This is what I have learned from these challenges. With my inner strength, my drive and determination, plus the support from the amazing legends around me, I am truly unstoppable and unbreakable.

*'BE YOU, BE PROUD AND BELIEVE IN YOURSELF. SHOW THE WORLD WHO YOU ARE.'*

*Salvatore Bruno*

My name is Salvatore Bruno and I am just a normal guy walking this planet, but when the time comes I use all my inner powers and I am proud to say that I do believe that I can achieve anything. Yes, I am Bruno, and I am the Mad Rider,

**Question:**

*What is your challenge going to be?*

# Chapter 23

# YOUR OWN BOOK OF LIFE!

So there you have it: my journey, my outlook on life, my challenges, and how I believe that you truly can do anything you want and you can make any dream a reality with a positive mindset.

Imagine a life where everything you want can be achieved if you have the right determination and willingness to put in the hard work. You know that times will be hard but you also know you will bounce back stronger, and better than ever. The only difference between me and you is that I have already made that decision to live life my way, to make it my own, and to make some epic memories along the way. I want to be able to open people's eyes to see the world through a set of positive eyes.

This is my book and my story, and I have told you the ins and outs of how I became the person I am today. I wanted to be honest with you all, so that you know you are not alone and that other people are struggling with life's path, desperate to get out of the same routine day in day out.

I am hoping that reading this book will have opened your eyes to how you can view life differently, see people for what they are, and how to overcome any situation life throws at you. Yes, this is my story, but the aim of this book was never about just telling my story. The purpose was to encourage you to go on and write your own book of life.

I want you to be able to look back in years to come and see all the amazing things you have achieved, all the positive things that surround you, and how every day is just another day closer to your dreams. I want you to walk with your head held high, showing the world that you are proud of who you are, and every time your feet hit the ground people can see that you mean business, and you are here to do things your way.

You have the tools now and you know that all you need lies within you. You just have to find your new path and unleash those inner strengths. So, spark up that inner furnace and let that power run through your veins, through each muscle, cell, and bone, as you grow into something you thought impossible. Watch as you become someone that others look to for support and guidance, see how others take motivation from you. You have been invited to come to join the superhumans of this world, and we are all waiting to welcome you.

The only thing you need to do now is make that decision. Do you go back to how things were, the normal routine, that job you hate, not having money, being overweight, whatever you are not happy with? These are all just choices, and you are the one that has to choose.

DO YOU WANT IT? DO YOU WANT TO BE BETTER?

If the answer is yes, then you are ready to make that next step. You are ready to wake up tomorrow and enjoy that different feeling. And as your life begins to look different, you will no longer seeing the negative parts in your world. You will see the sunrise and notice the positives out there which are drawing you in. They will help you to walk away from the grey parts of your life and head towards a brighter, more positive future.

You are ready to start your book of life, to write about the amazing journeys you will take, and the epic memories you will make. The most important part of your book is how you grow into a much better version of yourself, are happier, more positive, and life feels the way you want it to be. Every book on life has to start somewhere. And although we may start this special journey at different ages or through different circumstances, we all still have to take that first step on our new path of life.

Your book starts now. Remove all the negatives from your past and use them as your fuel to start moving forward in a different direction, a better direction, one where you are in control and no longer just going along for the ride.

This is your choice, your drive, your deter-mination, and your outlook on a new and better life. This is you wanting to live the life you dreamed about. So picture it, imagine the moment that you say enough is enough and you take that deep breath, you look up from the ground, and see what is in front of you and where you are heading next.

You then exhale as you lift your foot slowly off the floor and start to take your very first step onto your new path. Your foot hits the ground and sends this feeling shooting through your legs and up into your body. Suddenly the internal furnace is lit, your adrenalin starts to make your body tingle, and you take another step. Now you are walking down your new positive path of life.

*'IF YOU EVER WALK DOWN A PATH SURROUNDED BY NEGATIVE ENERGY, LOOK FOR THE FORK IN THE PATH AND CROSS OVER TO THE POSITIVE SIDE.'*
*Salvatore Bruno*

Start by doing what is necessary, then do what's possible, and suddenly you find are doing the impossible. Tell yourself that you can, believe in your ability, and let that inner strength blast out as the look in your eyes changes. Anyone who looks into them will see the internal fire glowing as positivity surrounds you. You can do this, so don't doubt yourself, believe in you, belief in what is possible, and then go make the impossible happen. Watch as page after page you start to write the most amazing story, one full of energy, motivation, determination, and positivity.

Watch as this book, your book, becomes a story which others will want to read and become a part of. Then suddenly your book of life is becoming your world – it's your past, your present, and your future; it's your dark days followed by your bright days.

It's about how negativity turned to positivity, and this amazing book becomes something you cherish and hold with pride. It has been written by your hard work; this book is who you are.

Make that step, put that pen to paper, and write these words…

'My name is …………… and this is my book of life, my past, my present, and my future.'

I have given you everything you need to start; all my tricks, tools, and even my story. I have even given you the first line to your book of life, so now it's time for me to pass it over to you. Take what I have given you and continue your own story – make an amazing story, an epic life, and all your dreams come to life.

*'YOUR PAST HAS ALREADY BEEN WRITTEN, BUT YOUR FUTURE CAN BE THE BEST STORY EVER. WRITE THE STORY YOU DREAM OF.'*
*Salvatore Bruno*

It's Time. Your Book, Your Life, Your Memories, Your Dreams, and simply YOUR CHOICE!

# Chapter 24

# I THANK YOU ALL!

I want to say a massive thank you to everyone who has been a part of me becoming who I am today. I am so lucky to have such amazing people around me, and that is super important to anyone's journey.

My journey is far from over and the best is yet to come, so I wanted to make sure those people understand how much I appreciate them, how they will always have a place in my heart.

There are other people's names that won't be mentioned, as they have impacted my life negatively. But that has made me into a better person also, so I also thank them.

I have learned from every life lesson, good or bad, so it's important to embrace those moments and understand that everything happens for a reason.

I stand in front of you all now, proud, positive, always ready to battle life and whatever it throws at me. I will continue to get my strength from the people around me and from the ones who are no longer with us.

I will never forget those people who crossed my path and have impacted me in a certain way. Good or bad, I use those memories to fuel my inner strengths to be a better son, partner, father, uncle, cousin, and friend. Whatever I am to you, I hope I do you proud, as I am eternally grateful for what you have given me and I promise that I will not stop improving and becoming the better version of myself.

So, to my partner, kids, family, friends, V2 team, and all those people who have been there when I needed them, I truly thank you x

I also have a special thank you for a certain few people who know I love them with all my heart and without whom I am truly nothing.

This MASSIVE thank you goes to:

**Rosita Bruno,** the most amazing mum I know. You're truly an incredibly strong woman, and the strength you have shown me is unreal.

**Sienna and Luca,** my children. I am blessed to have you and you really have no idea how much determination you give me. We truly have an unbreakable connection.

**David and Linda,** my brother and sister. It's been a hell of a journey and I couldn't have done it without you two. I am super proud to call myself your big bro.

**Karolina Jurkiewicz**, my partner in crime, my beauty, my business partner, and my better half. You have been absolutely unbelievable. How you put up with me, I have no idea, I couldn't do this without you. We are solid and love smashing our dreams together.

And...

**Carlo Bruno**, my father, the legend of all legends, my rock, the inspiration for this book, the reason I perform my challenges, plus a huge part of why I am the person I am today. You have shown me in the past so many things, but the things you continue to show me from the shadows are even more powerful.

Life has not been the same since you passed, but I know you are there. I feel you, and I will stick to my promise. You truly are my hero, and I thank you for everything. I am proud to call myself your son.

And my final thank you goes to you all. Thank you for taking the time to be a part of my life by reading my book. It's because of legends like you that we can grow and continue to learn, and I hope very soon I will be able to shake your hand and say thank you in person.

Smile, be proud, and Live Life Your Way!

Love to you all,

Bruno,
aka The Mad Rider

*Book brought to you by Version2 Fitness*

# MESSAGE TO MY FATHER

My father Carlo Bruno – forever in my heart, and forever lighting up my darkest moments of my life – I will always love you and never forget what you have taught me. I promised you something, and I will not stop until I have made that come true.

You will forever be my rock and my hero, and you will always be the one who showed me the true meaning of life.

Forever grateful,

your son,

xxx

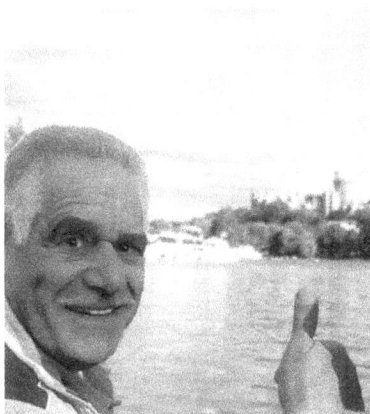

This book is in memory of my rock,

my hero, my father.

Carlo Bruno

9th March, 1949–2nd March, 2015

*Sara Sempre Nei Nostri Cuori*